Possum and Ole Ez
in the Public Eye

Possum and Ole Ez
in the Public Eye

Contemporaries and Peers on
T. S. Eliot and Ezra Pound
1892–1972

Burton Raffel

ARCHON BOOKS
1985

First published 1985 as an Archon Book,
an imprint of The Shoe String Press, Inc.,
Hamden, Connecticut 06514

Composition by The Publishing Nexus Incorporated
1200 Boston Post Road, Guilford, Connecticut 06437

Printed in the United States of America

The paper in this books meets the guidelines
for permanence and durability of the
Committee on Production Guidelines for Book Longevity
of the Council on Library Resources

Library of Congress Cataloging in Publication Data
Raffel, Burton.
   Possum and ole Ez in the public eye

   Bibliography: p.
   Includes index.
   1. Eliot, T. S. (Thomas Stearns), 1888-1965—Allusions.
2. Pound, Ezra, 1885-1972—Allusions. 3. Eliot, T. S. (Thomas
Stearns), 1888-1965—Friends and associates. 4. Pound, Ezra,
1885-1972—Friends and associates. 5. Poets, American—20th
century—Biography—Addresses, essays, lectures. I. Title.
PS3509.L43Z8156 1985   811'.52'09 [B]   84-24593
ISBN 0-208-02057-8

Contents

Part I
Introduction

I

This is not a collection of criticism: most of the writers whose comments appear here are neither academicians nor professional critics, nor are their concerns in these comments basically critical. The chronological record here set out is by and large a montage built out of writers' comments, some friendly, some unfriendly, as those writers reacted, year by year, to the work, the personalities, and the lives of two of the most important figures of twentieth-century letters. Both T. S. Eliot, who seems to have been given the private name of "Possum" by Ezra Pound, and Pound himself, who was throughout his life called all sorts of names, in public as well as in private, occupied for roughly half a century positions of intense visibility. Their importance far transcended strictly literary matters, though each of them exercised and continue still to exercise immense influence on other writers, mostly younger writers but also some their own age and even some older (and as eminent, in Pound's case, as William Butler Yeats).

What is attempted here, accordingly, is a succession of rapid and on the whole quite short glimpses of literary reputation as it was constituting and reconstituting itself. We see, for example, Leo Stein (Gertrude's brother) observing as late as mid-1934, when Eliot's reputation was already so formidable that some younger poets were feeling oppressed and even in part suppressed by it, that "I entertain ... grave doubts whether that book of T. S. Eliot's was worth the freight charges" required to send it. (All material quoted in this introductory essay is from the text of the book that follows.) That

3

same year W. B. Yeats, who never quite cottoned to Eliot or to his poetry, is seen confessing, albeit reluctantly, that Eliot "represents a movement that has grown all over the world and is strong at the Universities." Indeed, so pervasive had Eliot's influence become that an obsessive like Delmore Schwartz seized upon Eliot's life, as well as his work, and constructed an entire mythology of it. "Of all his literary heroes," records his biographer, James Atlas, "none was the object of a more merciless array of fabricated anecdotes than T. S. Eliot, whose every secret Delmore pretended to know." That process of mythicization was well underway by 1938. But even sixteen years earlier the novelist John Dos Passos was warning his friend, John Peale Bishop, that a new poem was "a little too Eliot." As early as 1920, well before *The Waste Land* exploded perhaps the largest poetic bombshell of our century (swelling Eliot's reputation immeasurably), the poet Hart Crane declared that "Eliot's influence threatens to predominate the new English."

There were to be sure dissenting voices. The pioneering critic, F. R. Leavis, records what happened to a young academic who ventured to speak his mind, and speak it favorably, on so heretical a theme. "When in 1929 an innocent young editor printed an article of mine on Mr. Eliot's criticism . . . he very soon had cause to realize that he had committed a scandalous impropriety, and I myself was left in no doubt as to the unforgiveableness of my offense." There were political dissenters as well as academic ones. Horace Gregory writes that about 1930 a Communist friend threw one of Eliot's books on the table, "saying he wouldn't keep such trash in the house." It surely did not help that the book was *For Lancelot Andrewes,* one of the fervently pietistic works of Eliot's first flush of religion. Troubled—one might almost say traumatized—poets like William Carlos Williams were proclaiming, by 1932, that "Eliot is finally and definitely dead—and his troop along with him." Almost a decade later another major poet, Wallace Stevens, declared with more truth as well as more balance: "It is possible that a man like T. S. Eliot illustrates the character [necessary to hold a chair of poetry], except that I regard him as a negative rather than a positive force."

Reactions to Pound—personally as well as literarily, for Pound seems quite deliberately to have made himself as well as

4

his work an issue—are similarly divided, though predictably a good deal more violent. His rather tepid first book, *A Lume Spento*, printed in Venice at Pound's own expense, was greeted in 1908 by such comments as "wild haunting stuff, absolutely poetic, original, imaginative, passionate and spiritual." Considering the general tepidity of the poetry then being written, especially in England, it is not entirely surprising to find the anonymous reviewer going on to observe that "Those who do not consider it crazy may well consider it inspired. Coming after the trite and decorous verse of most of our decorous poets, this poet seems like a minstrel of Provence"—which was of course exactly how Pound wanted to be seen. But other reviews of even that first book were not quite so enthusiastic. "The academician bristles all over his work.... He affects obscurity and loves the abstruse," said another critic, also anonymous. "We can find nothing but evidence of a highly interesting personality unable to express itself," declared still another unsigned review.

By 1910 one of Americas poetic fashion-makers, William Stanley Braithwaite, whose annual *Anthology of Magazine Verse* appeared from 1913 to 1929, felt sufficiently threatened by Pound's growing reputation and influence to snarl: "We began the examination of this book of poems with great expectations and we lay it down with considerable contempt for the bulk of English criticism that has pretended to discover in these erratic utterances the voice of a poet." An infinitely more positive commentator, Frank Steward Flint—a close friend and comrade-in-arms of Pound's—found in Pound's *Exultations* "a rift of real, though vague beauty, impalpable gold." And an anonymous critic affirmed that, in *Personae* and in *Exultations*, "Mr. Pound has given the vessel of poetry a rather violent shaking, but we are thankful to him for it, even though many dregs should be brought to the surface."

These splits in opinion grew sharper, rather than easing, over the years. By 1918 the poet Conrad Aiken wrote of *Pavannes and Divisions*, a volume of prose, that its "outstanding feature ... is its dullness.... It is ugliness and awkwardness incarnate." Since Aiken was a novelist as well as a poet, the criticism is all the more barbed. Virginia Woolf's nastiness was totally unprincipled: "Not that I've read more than 10 words by Ezra Pound," she wrote to Roger Fry, also in 1918, "but my

5

conviction of his humbug is unalterable." Pound's good friend, T. S. Eliot, declared in that same year of the same book Aiken had condemned: "Whether we agree or not with his opinions, we may be always sure that ... he is not to be diverted on any pretext from the essential literary problem, that he is always concerned with the work of art, never with incidental fancies." And the next year Hart Crane confessed to Gorham Munson that "More and more am I turning toward Pound and Eliot and the minor Elizabethans for values." In 1920 the poet and novelist, May Sinclair, spoke of "the clear hardness, the civilised polished beauty, the Augustan irony of Ezra Pound."

It was a split that grew steadily worse rather than better. Pound's onetime friend, the embittered poet, John Gould Fletcher, explained in 1929 that "No one with an open mind can possibly read Mr. Pound's poetry without realizing that he is above all, a traditionalist." Such a label applied to the author of *Make It New*, always a self-proclaimed radical, was a deliberate and rather snide insult. But Fletcher had still more insults: "To say that they [the *Cantos*] are a poem in any sense of the word is to say that calisthenics are essentially the same thing as the Russian ballet." Two years later Allen Tate wrote that Pound's poetry "has had more influence on us than any other of our time"; the next year Ernest Hemingway roared that "Any poet born in this century or in the last ten years of the preceding century who can honestly say that he has not been influenced by or learned greatly from the work of Ezra Pound deserves to be pitied rather than rebuked." At the same time the poet Archibald MacLeish was telling Louis Untermeyer that "Pound is a unicorn who turns into an ass every time you look at him too closely." In 1936 Yeats summed up a lifetime of trying to deal with Pound by observing, as ever somewhat uncomfortably, that "especially when he is writing in *vers libre* ... he has not got all the wine into the bowl," and in 1938 Robert Frost rather similarly sighed, "Poor Ezra.... Such travesties of what we have desired take the spirit out of my old age more than all that can be called defeat. They give me that what's-the-use feeling." That same year James Laughlin asserted: "Only Yeats and Eliot can compare with Pound among living poets for richness of diction." Dudley Fitts affirmed, the next year, that "he has a better ear, a subtler, more assured feeling for language, than anyone writing today."

Pound's wartime broadcasts from Rome, collected in 1978 as the distinctly sickening volume "*Ezra Pound Speaking*", led to his arrest, indictment, and eventual longtime incarceration in the mental ward of a Washington, D.C. hospital—and the fuss and flap *that* produced came close to making the earlier divisions of opinion look minor and relatively benign. This late phase of Pound's career was capped, in a sense, by the award of the Bollingen Prize, in 1949, for his 1948 volume, *The Pisan Cantos*. Outcry and counter-outcry followed, as virtually everyone who was anyone in the literary world (as also in the political word) felt impelled to speak his or her piece.

II

This chronological record of their peers' and their contemporaries' reactions offers a somewhat different perspective on the lives and especially on the careers of T. S. Eliot and Ezra Pound. There are things to be learned, here, that more formal critical writing either does not deal with at all or else deals with only in extremely different lights and, at best, very partially. (There are, incidentally, things to be learned, too, about the writers of these comments, who often reveal quite as much about themselves as they do about the subjects they are nominally addressing.) But there is I think a larger value in this record, namely a useful practical demonstration of just what literary "reputation" means.

We tend to think of reputation in taxonomic rather than dynamic terms—that is, we tend to see reputation either as something fixed and settled for all eternity or else as something with fairly well defined stages, each relatively self-contained and above all pretty neatly definable. We are startled, perhaps, to learn that Shakespeare—today held to be without question the king of literary kings—was in some earlier periods regarded as something of a primitive, even a slightly barbarous primitive. John Dryden, for example, though he regarded Shakespeare as "incomparable," also declared in 1668 that the incomparable one nevertheless "did not perfectly observe the laws of comedy," meaning the laws laid down by the Ancients. Additionally, despite "the largest and most com-

7

prehensive soul," Dryden felt obliged to admit that Shakespeare "is many times flat, insipid; his comic wit degenerating into clenches, his serious welling into bombast." Not only did Dryden proceed to rewrite *The Tempest*, to iron out such crudities, but at a later point also redid *Anthony and Cleopatra*, explaining with decorous condescension that "'tis almost a miracle that much of his language remains so pure; and that he who began dramatic poetry amongst us, untaught by any and, as Ben Johnson tells us, without learning, should by the force of his own genius perform so much that in a manner he has left no praise for any who come after him." Dryden's admiration for Shakespeare is no clearer than his conviction of Shakespeare's relatively unpolished qualities.

Dryden himself took his lumps, in the nineteenth century particularly. We esteem him as one of the major poets in the language. Not so, said Wordsworth: "I admire his talents and genius greatly, but he is not a poetical genius." Wordsworth's friend Southey, similarly, declared that "Dryden . . . lowered its [poetry's] tone, even while he improved the style of versification." Matthew Arnold, later in the nineteenth century (1880), went a good deal farther. "Though they may write in verse, though they may in a certain sense be masters of the art of versification, Dryden and Pope are not classics of our poetry, they are classics of our prose." As regards Dryden such an extreme judgement seems, to our time, rather difficult to understand—but applied to one of the greatest masters of English verse, Alexander Pope, it seems downright incomprehensible.

There are a host of similar examples of the *bouleversement* of reputation, over time. John Donne is a particularly well-known instance. "Towards the end of the seventeenth-century," notes Hugh Sykes Davis, editor of a fascinating two-volume anthology, *The Poets and Their Critics*, "Donne became the stock example of a man whose wit (whatever that meant from one time to another) was greater than his poetry, and whose versification was lamentable." "Would not Donne's *Satires*, which abound with so much wit," asked Dryden in 1693, "appear more charming, if he had taken care of his words, and of his numbers [versification]?" Ben Johnson's condemnation in 1619, "That Donne, for not keeping of accent, deserved hanging," can be written off as the sniping of a philosophical opponent, but Pope's remark that "Donne had no imagination, but as much wit, I think, as any writer can possibly have," fairly represents what the passing of a century had witnessed, the decline in reputation of Donne from a major to a distinctly minor poet. By 1839 Hallam could sneer: "Donne is the most inharmonious of our versifiers, if he can be said to have deserved such a name.... Few [of his poems] are good for much; the conceits have not even the merit of being intelligible; it would perhaps be difficult to select three passages that we chould care to read again." As late as 1899 Edmund Gosse could refer to "the remarkably wide and deep, though almost entirely malign, influence of Donne upon the poetry of this country." By 1931 the tables had once again been turned, and T. S. Eliot, who had a good deal to do with revitalizing Donne's poetic standing, could resoundingly affirm that "Donne ought always to be recognized as one of the few greeat reformers and preservers of the English tongue."

It would not be hard to multiply examples. Mad Christopher Smart is today far more esteemed than at any other period; the once massive figure of Waltor Savage Landor is today reduced to a kind of footnote to W. B. Yeats; Spenser's *The Fairy Queen*, which so delighted Wordsworth and his friends that they read it aloud by the hour, and the hour, and the hour, is today admired, if at all, largely as a historical artifact, and except by devoted scholars is very little read; Sir Phillip Sidney could find "great wants" in Chaucer, adding that to be sure such deficiencies were "fit to be forgiven in so reverent antiquity"—that is, Chaucer wrote so long ago that necessarily he could not have known what he was about.

Rather than discuss the history of particular reputations, however, let me use these and the preceding particularized illustrations to point up my observation that we tend to see literary reputation as a taxonomic process rather than as a dynamic one. For Chaucer, for Shakespeare, even for so relatively recent a poet as John Donne, we are of course lacking in much of the contemporary evidence, with which alone a dynamic sense of how a poet was regarded in his own time, by his peers and colleagues, can be recovered. Beginning with John Milton, and certainly by the time of William Blake and the later Romantics, the evidence is reasonably full and a dynamic presentation well within reach.

What a dynamic presentation can offer is something at least of what it was actually like, at any particular moment, to be alive and reading, say, a master work like *The Waste Land* as it was first appearing on the literary horizon. It is not nasty, nor ought we so to view it, when Hart Crane in 1922 writes that he was "rather disappointed" in the poem. "It was good, of course, but so damned dead." It is not superficial but importantly revealing to learn that Edith Wharton felt the poem "to lack even the enlivening presence of Walt Whitman; it was a poem, like Joyce's novel [*Ulysses*], ridden by theory rather than warmed by life." These are important comments, not because they reveal our immense superiority to these benighted, deluded folk, but because they reveal more fully than second-hand comment can the contemporary ground on which Eliot had to build his poetic edifice. They show us with a special amplitude, as well as with a special resonance, where poetry was when Eliot (with Pound's help) produced *The Waste Land*, and in so doing they help us better to understand what Eliot was up to, and a special aspect of what he was up against. Virginia Woolf's perceptive comment (she liked Eliot personally, which surely helped), after hearing Eliot read the poem, also underlines what was truly new—new, let me emphasize, *at that time*—about *The Waste Land*: "I have only the sound of it in my ears ... and have not yet tackled the sense. But I like the sound." Ernest Hemingway "was unable to take it seriously": that too is an important reflection of the time (and of Hemingway himself). Even seven years after the poem's publication, Dylan Thomas, linking Eliot and James Joyce, was referring to "their succession of sordid details, their damp despondent atmosphere, and their attraction for the gutter." Reinterpretation, a constantly renewed (and a constantly different) understanding, was going on all the time. Witness Lawrence Durrell's 1938 observation that while "today all writing is pretending to be Classical ... the origins of it are really ROMANTIC. Compare *Waste Land* with Baudelaire." Witness especially William Carlos William's staggered dismay at "the blast of Eliot's genius which gave the poem back to the academics. We did not know how to answer.... [It] drove me mad. I have never quite got over it." How much of the later history of Williams's poetry in particular, but also of much modern

10

poetry generally, is implied and to an extent explained in that passionate outburst of despair?

III

I do not want to claim too much for my collection of reactions and responses. I have been assiduous, turning over literally hundreds of books, hunting for revelatory material. But inevitably there must be more, perhaps even a great deal more, that I have not been able to find. I have recently written critical books on both Eliot and Pound; I have tried not to turn this book into an extended footnote to either of those volumes. No particular stance or approach has been intended (at least consciously). I have tried to be as objective as humanly possible, including invective and praise in the proportions in which I found them. It matters not a bit, for my purposes here, whether a writer's comments are right or wrong, but only that they were made and that they reflect something that seems significant and worth our attention. I would be grateful to be notified of omissions of any sort, as also I welcome corrections of any sort. I cannot promise to respond individually to any and all such transmissions, but I can and do promise to consider them with the respectful seriousness they deserve.

Part II
T. S. Eliot

T. S. Eliot
A Brief Chronology

1888	Born on 26 September in St. Louis, Missouri
c. 1895–1906	Attends private schools
1906–1910	Attends Harvard, takes B.A. in 1909, M.A. in 1910
1910–1911	Attends the Sorbonne, Paris
1911–1914	Graduate work in philosophy at Harvard; completes course work for Ph.D.; begins dissertation on F. H. Bradley
1914–1915	Attends Marburg University, Germany, and Oxford University, England
1915–1916	Marries Vivienne Haigh-Wood; teaches school; finishes dissertation, which is approved
1917–1925	Employed at Lloyds Bank
1917	Publishes *The Love Song of J. Alfred Prufrock and Other Observations*
1917–1919	Assistant editor of *The Egoist*
1919	Publishes (with the Hogarth Press of Leonard and Virginia Woolf) *Poems 1919*
1920	Publishes *Poems, 1920* and *The Sacred Wood*
1922	Publishes *The Waste Land*; becomes founding editor of *The Criterion*
1925	Eliot and *The Criterion* join what later became the publishing firm of Faber and Faber; publishes "The Hollow Men"

1927	Becomes Anglo-Catholic and British citizen
1928	Publishes *For Lancelot Andrewes*, preface affirming him "classicist...royalist...anglo-catholic"
1930	Publishes *Ash-Wednesday*
1932	Publishes *Selected Essays*
1932	Publishes *The Use of Poetry & the Use of Criticism*
1934	*The Rock* performed; publishes *After Strange Gods*
1935	Publishes *Burnt Norton*; *Murder in The Cathedral* performed.
1939	*The Family Reunion* performed; publishes *Old Possum's Book of Practical Cats* and *The Idea of a Christian Society*
1940	Publishes *Eask Coker*
1941	Publishes *The Dry Salvages*
1942	Publishes *Little Gidding*
1947	Vivienne Eliot dies
1948	Awarded the Nobel Prize
1949	Publishes *Notes Toward a Definition of Culture*
1950	*The Cocktail Party* performed
1957	Marries Valerie Fletcher
1959	*The Elder Statesman*, his last play, is performed
1965	Dies on 4 January

1913

In 1913, the Cambridge Dramatic Club ... produced Jerome K. Jerome's *Fanny and the Servant Problem*—in which Cummings was cast as Micah, the second footman. Of this production ... he recalls two things: that he was kissed 'by the very beautiful leading lady', and that the hero, 'Lord Somebody or Other', was brilliantly played by a 'cold and aloof' person. This person was T. S. Eliot.

Charles Norman, *E. E. Cummings*, pp. 33–34

1916

You ought to read his [Eliot's] things. They are all the more remarkable when one knows the man, ordinarily just an Europeanized American, overwhelmingly cultured, talking about French literature in the most uninspired fashion imaginable.

Aldous Huxley to Julian Huxley, 29 December 1916

1917

I've asked the poet T. S. Eliot to dine with me ... and he's a very nice creature.

Aldous Huxley to Naomi Mitchison, May 1917

From there I whisked to lunch with Lady Tredegar and after that to Eliot, whom I found haggard and ill-looking as usual; we held a council of war about a poetry reading, in which both of us are supposed to be performing to-morrow ...

Aldous Huxley to Juliette Baillot, 11 December 1917

But oh—what a performance: Eliot and I were the only people who had any dignity ...

Aldous Huxley to Julian Huxley, 13 December 1917

17

1918

We've been having that strange young man Eliot to dinner. His sentences take such an enormous time to spread themselves out that we didn't get very far; but we did reach Ezra Pound and Wyndham Lewis, and how they were great geniuses, and so is Mr. James Joyce—which I'm more prepared to agree to, but why has Eliot stuck in this mud? Can't his culture carry him through, or does culture land one there?

Virginia Woolf to Roger Fry, 18 November 1918

I went over to Marlow the other day and saw Eliot and his wife who have taken a house there. Eliot in excellent form and his wife too; I rather like her; she is such a genuine person, vulgar, but with no attempt to conceal her vulgarity ...

Aldous Huxley to Julian Huxley, 28 June 1918

You hear poor Eliot has been called up and will probably be a private in the Kentucky Yeomanry or the Memphis, Ohio, Fusiliers in a month's time? It's too deplorable. I hope something can be done for him.

Aldous Huxley to J. C. Squire, August 1918

I saw Eliot last week in London and had a delightful literary talk with him. He has published three or four new poems in the *Little Review*, two of which are interesting, the others not. He is, I think, very remarkable. Also very charming.

Aldous Huxley to Julian Huxley, 20 November 1918

1918/1922

In the strange, violent world created by the war new movements were a-borning, new literary high priests emerging: the Sitwells, T. S. Eliot, Aldous Huxley. Four momentous years of war had considerably changed the tone of literary London.

Robert H. Ross, *The Georgian Revolt*, p. 167

1919

Of the poets you mention (those among them whose work I know at any rate) [Jack] Lindsay and Eliot seem to me to be the only live writers.
> Edith Sitwell to Robert Nichols, March 1919

T. S. Eliot, Maupassant and *The L[ittle] R[eview]* have been my steady companions.
> Hart Crane to Gorham Munson, 22 November 1919

More and more am I turning toward Pound and Eliot and the minor Elizabethans for values.
> Hart Crane to Gorham Munson, 27 December 1919

He [Eliot]'s greatly improved—far more self-assured, decidedly intelligent, and, so far as I could see, nice.... Poet Eliot had dinner with me on Monday—rather ill and rather American: altogether not quite gay enough for my taste. But by no means to be sniffed at.... I do like him, though. He's changed a great deal since I last saw him—a long time ago. But the devitalisation I'm afraid may lead to disappointments.
> Lytton Strachey, quoted in Michael Holroyd,
> *Lytton Strachey: The Years of Achievement*, p. 364

1920

...Before an Eliot we become alive or intense as we become intense or alive before a Cézanne...
> E. E. Cummings, *A Miscellany Revised*, p. 26

If you come on Sunday I can offer as bait the presence of T. S. Eliot, the poet, who will be staying the weekend with my friends the Morrells here.
> Aldous Huxley to B. G. Brooks, 30 July 1920

Eliot's influence threatens to predominate the new English.
> Hart Crane to Gorham Munson, 13 October 1920

1921

Early in the year he read a collection of essays, *The Sacred Wood*, by a little-known writer named T. S. Eliot, and another...by George Santayana...Eliot came off better, he thought, because he had had the benefit of leaving America. He found the 'concentrated prose' of Eliot's book—'every sentence a riddle'—easier to read. 'T. S. Eliot hits the nail on the head and does so at once, Santayana after many trials.' Both men wrote 'American'— 'but *Eliot has lived in England*. The American intellect has a taste for 'floundering about'.'

> J. B. Yeats, quoted in William M. Murphy,
> *Prodigal Father: The Life of John Butler Yeats*, p. 524.

...am shocked as usual, when I read Eliot, to find how wrong I am, and how right he is...I'm sure he's wrong; and I shall perk up again, but what a shock it is. I think he's a Puritan, as well as an American.

> Virginia Woolf to Sydney Waterlow, 3 May 1921

It was apparently some sort of Poetry Society. There was ...Eliot—very sad and seedy—it made one weep...The rooms were peculiarly disgusting, and the company very miscellaneous....Why, oh why, does Eliot have any truck with such coagulations? I fear it indicates that there's something seriously wrong with him.

> Lytton Strachey, quoted in Michael Holroyd,
> *Lytton Strachey: The Years of Achievement*, p. 440.

1922

Last night Bunny [Edmund] Wilson and Elinor Wylie were reading your new poem...I thought it a little too Eliot— particularly the mannerism of using proper names of a baroque and yiddish character.

> John Dos Passos to John Peale Bishop, October 1922

In November, the magazine [*The Dial*] printed T. S. Eliot's *The Waste Land*, which prompted Amy to write [Gilbert] Seldes [editor of *The Dial*] that, though she found 'interesting passages' in it, the work as a whole left her cool . . . she said it was as if Eliot 'had laid a fire with infinite care but omitted to apply a match to it.'

Jean Gould, Amy [Lowell] p. 327

The publication of T. S. Eliot's 'The Waste Land' in the *Dial* was an explosion even more devastating than the magazine's revelation of the work of Thomas Mann. Arguments over the poem were endless, . . . yet one thing was made clear: students who argued over Eliot were certain that Swinburne's and Pater's 'paganism' had dropped out of date—even 'Satanism' at its 1890 naughtiest had suddenly acquired a hangdog, old-fashioned air.

Horace Gregory, The House on Jefferson Street, p 126

Edith Wharton found . . . [*Prufrock*] extremely 'amusing' . . . . but relatively insignificant and interesting mainly as revealing the influence of Whitman . . . *The Waste Land* . . . . seemed to her to lack even the enlivening presence of Walt Whitman; it was a poem, like Joyce's novel [*Ulysses*], ridden by theory rather than warmed by life.

R. W. B. Lewis, Edith Wharton, p. 442

I expect you're rather hard on Tom Eliots poem [*The Waste Land*]. I have only the sound of it in my ears, when he read it aloud; and have not yet tackled the sense. But I like the sound.

Virginia Woolf to David Garnett, 20 October 1922

What you say about Eliot does not surprise me . . . I have been facing him for *four* years,—and while I haven't discovered a weak spot yet in his armour, I flatter myself a little lately that I have discovered a safe tangent to strike which, if I can possibly explain the position,—goes *through* him toward a *different goal*. You see it is such a fearful temptation to imitate him that at times I have been almost distracted. . . . You will profit by reading him again and again. . . . In his own realm Eliot presents us with an absolute *impasse*, yet oddly enough, he can be utilized to lead us to, intelligently point to, other positions and 'pastures new'. Having absorbed him enough we can trust ourselves as never before . . .

Hart Crane to Allen Tate, 12 June 1922

What do you think of Eliot's *The Wasteland*? I was rather disappointed. It was good, of course, but so damned dead. Neither does it, in my opinion, add anything important to Eliot's achievement.

Hart Crane to Gorham Munson, 20 November 1922

'When *The Waste Land* appeared, complete with notes, E. E. Cummings asked me [Malcolm Cowley] why Eliot couldn't write his own lines instead of borrowing from dead poets. . . . The seven-page appendix to *The Waste Land* . . . was a painful dose for us to swallow. But the truth was that the poet had not changed so much as his younger readers. We were becoming less preoccupied with technique and were looking for poems that portrayed our own picture of the world. . . . . [Eliot] was saying that the present was inferior to the past . . . [and] we were excited by the adventure of living in the present'.

Malcolm Cowley, quoted in Charles Norman,
E. E. Cummings, pp. 150–151

1923

Ezra [Pound] lent Ernest a copy of T. S. Eliot's new poem, *The Waste Land* . . . Ernest was unable to take it seriously . . .

Carlos Baker, *Ernest Hemingway*, p. 107

There is no one writing in English who can command so much respect, to my mind, as Eliot. However, I take Eliot as a point of departure toward an almost complete reverse of direction. His pessimism is amply justified, in his own case. But I would apply as much of his erudition and technique as I can absorb and assemble toward a more positive...goal....I feel that Eliot ignores certain spiritual events and possibilities as real and powerful as, say, in the time of Blake. Certainly the man has dug the ground and buried hope as deep and direfully as it can ever be done. He has outclassed Baudelaire with a devastating humor that the earlier poet lacked.

Hart Crane to Gorham Munson, 5 January 1923

I think Mr. Eliot conceived 'The Waste Land' out of an extremity of tragic emotion and expressed it in his own voice and the voices of other unhappy men not carefully and elaborately trained in close harmony, but coming as a confused and frightening and beautiful murmur out of the bowels of the earth....If it were merely a piece of virtuosity it would remain astonishing....But it is far more than this; it is infused with spirit and passion and despair...That he expresses the emotion of an intellectual is perfectly true, but of the intensity of that emotion there is, to my mind, no question, nor do I recognize any reason for such a question.

Elinor Wylie, quoted in Stanley Olson,
Elinor Wylie, p. 210

I think you'll find, if the arrangement can be worked, that Eliot has great influence with the younger writers, and would give the literary side of the Nation much more character than any of the ordinary literary hacks.

Virginia Woolf to John Maynard Keynes,
24 February 1923

That strange figure Eliot dined here last night. I feel that he has taken the veil, or whatever monks do....Tom, though infinitely considerate [of his wife], is also perfectly detached. His cell, is I'm sure, a very lofty one, but a little chilly. We have the oddest conversations: I can't help loosing some figure of speech, which Tom pounces upon and utterly destroys.

Virginia Woolf to Roger Fry, 18 May 1923

Last night, dining in high society, I sat next a young Lord at Oxford who said that Mr Eliot was his favorite poet, and the favorite of all his friends.... Mr Eliot's poems, he said, amused him more than anybodies, though he found them very difficult.

Virginia Woolf to T. S. Eliot, 4 June 1923

All marked styles are to be avoided, I think [in *The Waste Land*], because they limit one. He begins to repeat himself. He creaks: he angles,...but I insist, against his many detractors that these are only the impediments of a very good brain.

Virginia Woolf to Gerald Brenan, 10 August 1923

1924

Tom has written, asking for news of Angelica; he has a good heart...

Virginia Woolf to Vanessa Bell, 27 April 1924

T. S. Eliot had come to Paris about then, appearing at the Dôme and other bars in top hat, cutaway, and striped trousers. It was intended as a gesture of contempt and received just that.

William Carlos Williams, *Autobiography* (quoting a diary entry), p. 217

'T. S. Eliot, poet-laureate and elegist of the jazz age'...

Burton Rascoe, quoted in Charles Norman, *E. E. Cummings*, pp. 189–190

Ernest was nearly as hard on T. S. Eliot, whom he persisted in calling 'The Major'. He alluded superciliously to the 'heavy uncut pages of Eliot's quarterly', the *Criterion*.... Ernest went out of his way to remark in print that if he could bring [Joseph] Conrad back to life 'by grinding Mr. Eliot into a fine dry powder and sprinkling that powder over Conrad's grave in Canterbury', he would 'leave for London early tomorrow morning with a sausage-grinder'.

Carlos Baker, *Ernest Hemingway*, p. 135

1925

Aldington has set his heart on making a journalist of Tom [Eliot], and as far as I can make out, they are now trying to get support for the Criterion and start him on that and any other odds and ends they can come by. It is not accomplished yet: and knowing Tom, perhaps never will be.... Don't I know that Tom lives in a *basement*, that his position is degrading, insecure, ruinous to his health, destructive of his writing.

Virginia Woolf to Mary Hutchinson, 16 February 1925

I still stick to the rags and tatters that remain (of Tom's character) with the tenacity of a leech, but get little help from Leonard. But suppose a little boy was beaten every day, and had his fingers shut in doors, and dead rats tied to his tail coat—that is Tom's predicament I maintain—he might fail in that manly and straightforward conduct which we all admire.

Virginia Woolf to Mary Hutchinson, 14 September 1925

1926

We stopped on the way at Oxford and bought a waistcoat and some books—including T. S. Eliot's poems which seem to me marvellously good but very hard to understand. There is a most impressive flavour of the major prophets about them.

Evelyn Waugh, *Diaries*, p. 242

Rimbaud was the last great poet that our civilization will see— he let off all the great cannon crackers in Valhalla's parapets, the sun has set theatrically several times since while Laforgue, Eliot and others of that kidney have whimpered fastidiously.

Hart Crane to Waldo Frank, 20 June 1926

Now, confidential: T. S. Eliot, for whom you know my profound admiration—I think he's the greatest living poet in any language—wrote me he'd read *Gatsby* three times and thought it was *the first step forward American fiction had taken since Henry James*.

F. Scott Fitzgerald to Maxwell Perkins, 20 February 1926

1927

I have been especially gratified by the reception afforded me by *The Criterion*, whose director, Mr. T. S. Eliot, is representative of the most exacting literary standards of our times.

Hart Crane to Otto H. Kahn, 12 September 1927

1928

...It was only to be expected that Mr [T. Sturge] Moore ... should darken with misinformation the ignorance of Mr [T. S.] Eliot.

A. E. Housman, letter to the
London *Times*, 13 December 1928

'the Literature of Nerves, established by T. S. Eliot's *Waste Land*' ...

S. Foster Damon, quoted in Charles Norman,
E. E. Cummings, p. 214

...only decorous visits—as from Tom for example, whose pomp was such, and innuendoes about Vivien's sanity, that we both guffawed behind our hands.

Virginia Woolf to Vanessa Bell, January 1928

Tomorrow we are ... going to the Eliots to discuss Tom's new poems; but not only that—to drink cocktails and play jazz into the bargain, Tom thinking one can't do anything simple. He thinks this makes the occasion modern, chic. He will, no doubt, be sick in the back room; we shall all feel ashamed of our species. He has written some new poems, religious, I'm afraid, and is in doubt about his soul as a writer.

Virginia Woolf to Roger Fry, 16 October 1928

The spiritual disintegration of our period becomes more pain-ful to me every day...In every quarter (Lewis, Eliot, Fernandez, etc.) a thousand issues are raised for one that is settled...

Hart Crane to Gorham Munson, 17 April 1928

There's nobody new to take our place as the younger poets: or so I heard them lamenting with a false note in the Mercury [magazine] office. The Sitwells and T. S. Eliot were pointedly left out of count.

> Robert Frost to Lesley Frost, 11 September 1928

1929

Assuming that no subject is an unpoetical subject, the neo-Romanticists (headed by T. S. Eliot, and, in the majority of his moments, by James Joyce) give us their succession of sordid details, their damp despondent atmosphere, and their atraction for the gutter . . .

> Dylan Thomas, quoted in Constantine Fitzgibbon,
> *The Life of Dylan Thomas*, p. 50

When in 1929 an innocent young editor printed an article of mine on Mr Eliot's criticism in the *Cambridge Review* (a reply to a contemptuous dismissal of him by a Cambridge 'English' don in Mr Desmond McCarthy's *Life and Letters*) he very soon had cause to realize that he had committed a scandalous impropriety, and I myself was left in no doubt as to the unforgivableness of my offense.

> F. R. Leavis, "Retrospect 1959,"
> in *New Bearings in English Poetry*, p. 176

1930

Dotty refused to publish him, for which I dont altogether blame her, seeing that his poems are steeped in Tom—a scent that sticks like the skunk or the musk and one can't smell any other.

> Virginia Woolf to Clive Bell, 6 February 1930

I also share your admiration for the poetry of Archibald Mac-Leish, though I feel that at times he betrays too evidently a bias toward the fashionable pessimism of the hour so well established by T. S. Eliot.

> Hart Crane to Selden Rodman, 22 May 1930

My summer was a kind of steady doldrums, enlivened only by a sudden insight into the values and beauty of Dante's *Commedia*. Not that I've learned Italian, but that I found a decent translation ... thanks to Eliot's inspiring essay on Dante.

Hart Crane to Solomon Grunberg, 30 September 1930

Delmore at seventeen was a self-styled member of the avant-garde; he read *Hound & Horn*, studied Pound's *Cantos* as they appeared, and collected first editions of everything T. S. Eliot wrote.

James Atlas, *Delmore Schwartz*, p. 38

1930[?]

[A Communist friend] threw the book [*For Lancelot Andrewes*] on the table, saying he wouldn't keep such trash in his house. I told him that I'd take it off his hands ... At the very least, Eliot put one's intelligence to work, and in his essays, since he had made an art of quoting poetry with startling effects, one was almost certain to discover new aspects of verse itself.

Horace Gregory, *The House on Jefferson Street*, p. 187

1931

It is my belief that, in a discussion of Eliot's poetry, his religious doctrines in themselves have little that commands interest.... His own failure to understand his position is irony, and the poet's insight into it is humility.... That is essentially the poetic attitude, an attitude that Eliot has been approaching with increasing purity. It is not that his recent verse is better than that of the period ending with *The Waste Land*. Actually it is less spectacular and less complex in subject matter ... His new form is simple, expressive, homogeneous, and direct, and without the early elements of violent contrast.

Allen Tate, *Essays of Four Decades*, pp. 462, 467

1932

Let us once and for all understand that Eliot is finally and definitely dead—and his troop along with him....[Eliot] is concerned with the line as it is modulated by a limited kind of half-alive speech.

> William Carlos Williams to Kay Boyle, quoted
> in *American Poetic Theory*, ed. George Perkins, pp. 265, 270

...he sits there, as trim as a bank clerk, making exact, but rather laboured conversation—for instance about his motor car. But as you've never seen him or read him this means less than nothing to you. Isnt it odd that you read Maurice Baring and not Tom Eliot?...I would give all MBs copious works for one of Tom's least and most brittle phrases.

> Virginia Woolf to Ethel Smyth, 7 September 1932

I larked...at a party where I met T. S. Eliot a month ago. He offered to read a poem if I would read one. I made him a counter-offer to *write* one while he was reading his. Then I fussed around with place-cards and a borrowed pencil, pretending an inspiration. When my time came...I did nine four-line stanzas...[which] I had composed...the summer before....I'm much to blame, but I just couldn't be serious when Eliot was taking himself so seriously.

> Robert Frost to Louis Untermeyer, 13 December 1932

Like most poets of his age in America, Crane discovered Rimbaud through Eliot and the Imagists...

> Allen Tate, *Essays of Four Decades*, p. 310

The followers of Eliot take his 'philosophy' as well as his style, and give us work of 'lower intensity' than the original....[But] it is a mistake to suppose that MacLeish has offered a 'way out' of the introspective indecision of the school of T. S. Eliot...

> Allen Tate, *Essays of Four Decades*, pp. 358, 360

But when all qualifications have been urged, *The Waste Land* remains a great positive achievement, and one of the first importance for English poetry. In it a mind fully alive in the age compels a poetic triumph out of the peculiar difficulties facing a poet in the age. And in solving his own problems as a poet Mr Eliot did more than solve the problem for himself. Even if *The Waste Land* had been, as used to be said, a 'dead end' for him, it would still have been a new start for English poetry.

F. R. Leavis, New Bearings in English Poetry, p. 95

1932/1933

Eliot arrived [for a poetry reading], in white-tie evening dress, ten minutes late: he was flushed and bright, and looked supremely exhilarated: he bowed to all of us and said, 'Forgive me, if I seem a bit post-war, but I'm rather tight. I have to prepare myself to face all those people. I always drink before reading poetry'. . . . I believe that Eliot actually dreaded mounting to the stage, but once he was there, he lived up to the occasion, and seemed to enjoy himself—moreover, he overwhelmed the crowd that heard him. Some few had come with the intention of heckling him, but he met the occasion with such well-poised levity that his enjoyment of the moment became contagious.

Horace Gregory, The House
on Jefferson Street, pp. 205–206

1933

The question is, will he [Eliot] drop Christianity with his wife, as one might empty the fishbones after the herring.

Virginia Woolf to Francis Birrell, 3 September 1933

He [Herbert Fisher] sniffs at Bloomsbury. 'No I cannot see much to be said for Mr Eliot; no music'. He thinks Winston Churchill a very good painter. He deplores the present state of everything.

Virginia Woolf to Quentin Bell, 3 December 1933

Thanks for your letter and the press cuttings [reviews of a lecture given by Housman]. I enclose another one, which is amusing, because its author, T. S. Eliot [who liked the lecture], is worshipped as a god by the writers in the paper which had the only hostile review.

A. E. Housman to Katharine Symons, 25 October 1933

T. S. Eliot seems to me a very great person.

F. Scott Fitzgerald to Mrs. Bayard Turnbull, Spring 1933

[Joyce's *Ulysses*] sums up better than any book I know the fearful despair that is almost normal in modern times. You get the same kind of things, though only just touched upon, in Eliot's poems. With E, however, there is also a certain sniffish 'I told you so' implication, because as the spoilt darling of the *Church Times* he is bound to point out that all this wouldn't have happened if we had not shut our eyes to the Light.

George Orwell to Brenda Salkeld, June 1933,
Collected Essays . . . , I:145

1934

I entertain . . . grave doubts whether that book of T. S. Eliot's was worth the freight charges. Apart from some of the comments on particular authors, it is for me entirely futile. Its one value may be that henceforth I shall avoid the books of the younger conservatives. . . . We have passed the time where naiveté in judgment, like Eliot's, is admissible. . . . Eliot was interesting when he had something to *say*. Now that he has something to *preach* he's a bore.

Leo Stein to Mabel Weeks, Summer 1934

In the last year or two owing to a nasty slap I got from an American follower of Eliot's, I confess I have several times forgotten my dignity in speaking in public of Eliot. I mean I have shown a hostility I should like to think in my pride unworthy of my position.... Pound really has great though inaccurate learning. Eliot has even greater.... Eliot has written in the throes of getting religion and forswearing a world gone bad with war. That seems deep. But I dont know.

Robert Frost to Lesley Frost Francis, 1934

I think I agree with your husband that a lot of people could have made up 'for fun' something better than Eliot's poem, but I want Eliot for the Mercury because he represents a movement that has grown all over the world and is strong at the Universities. It seeks modernness in language and metaphor and helps us to get rid of what Rossetti called 'soulless self-reflections of man's skill' but it does throw out the baby with the bath-water.

W. B. Yeats to Margot Ruddock, 17 November 1934

The rock [T. S. Eliot] disappointed me. I couldn't go and see it ... and in reading, without seeing, perhaps one got the horror of that cheap farce and Cockney dialogue and dogmatism too full in the face. Roger Fry, though, went and came out in a rage. But I thought even the choruses tainted; and rather like an old ship swaying in the same track as the Waste Land—a repetition, I mean. But I cant be sure that I wasn't unfairly influenced by my anti-religious bias. He seems to me to be petrifying into a priest—poor old Tom.

Virignia Woolf to Stephen Spender, 10 July 1934

And, best of all, T. S. Eliot wants me to call & see him. He was, for him, quite complimentary.

Dylan Thomas to Pamela Hansford Johnson,
28 March 1934

Others, like Eliot, have become so aware of the huge mechanism of the past that their poems read like scholarly conglomerations of a century's wisdom, and are difficult to follow unless we have an intimate knowledge of Dante, the Golden Bough, and the weather-reports in Sanskrit.

Dylan Thomas to Glyn Jones, 16 March 1934

Eliot . . . seemed younger than when I had first met him in New York—more sensitive, more volatile, more alert. . . . Years later, when I saw *The Cocktail Party* in New York, I realized that the side of Eliot that was uppermost in that Soho [London] restaurant resembled Sir Henry Harcourt-Reilly, the victorious, lighthearted psychiatrist of the play . . . He later asserted that the most heinous crime a writer could commit was dullness . . . Eliot remarked that . . . pedantry and rules were not for him—that though he could never write a poem without the music of it running through his head, he could never remember the laws of scanning verse—the melodic theme of the poem was the thing!

Horace Gregory, The House
on Jefferson Street, pp. 226–224

1935

I am trying to understand for the sake of my *Cambridge* [*sic*] *Book of Modern Verse* the Auden, Eliot school. I do not mean to give it a great deal of space, but must define my objections to it, and I cannot know this till I see clearly what quality it has [that has] made it delight young Cambridge and young Oxford.

W. B. Yeats to Margot Ruddock, 25 February 1935

It is, I think, interesting to observe that in [John Peale] Bishop two contemporary influences, Yeats and Eliot, meet strongly, and meet only in him of all the contemporary poets whom I know anything about: Yeats for form, Eliot for the experiment in language.

Allen Tate, Essays of Four Decades, p. 352

We had old Tom to stay the week end; he was urbanity itself...He's determined to write plays about modern life in verse, and rather crusty when reviewers say he's an old fogy. In fact I think he feels that hes only just beginning to write what he wants.

Virginia Woolf to Julian Bell, 14 October 1935

...put some red blood into that lily livered man [Eliot]. I went to his play [*Murder in the Cathedral*] last night, and came away as if I'd been rolling in the ash bin; and somehow filled my mouth with the bones of a decaying cat thrown there by a workhouse drab.

Virginia Woolf to Ethel Smyth, 13 November 1935

No, my criticism of the Murder was a violent flare, not to be taken as serious criticism. Though violent flares are always good evidence. The truth is it acts far less well than reads: cant manage the human body: only a soliloquy

Virginia Woolf to Ethel Smyth, 16 November 1935

I have just read the unpublished poems of a young man called Thomas Driberg. They seem to me to show really remarkable promise, and, at moments, achievement. he is very greatly under your influence (though not in form; he needs more shaping). But then, who is not?

Edith Sitwell to T. S. Eliot, 26 June 1935

Here is T. S. Eliot on the servnt-problem as seen from the Anglo-Catholic standpoint: 'I do not like the situation (i.e. of having only one servant)....I should prefer to employ a large staff of servants, each doing lighter work but profiting by the benefits of the cultured and devout atmosphere of the home in which they lived.' That bit about the cultured and devout atmosphere reminds me, as Samuel Butler said of a cracked church bell he heard somewhere, of the smell of a bug.

George Orwell to Brenda Salkeld, 7 March 1935, *Collected Essays* . . . , I:175

Eliot was getting some money together to help a young poet called George Barker; not only did Ottoline give generously, she also worked on Barker's behalf for several years.

Sandra Jobson Darroch, *Ottoline*, p. 256

[In] *After Strange Gods* ... Mr. Eliot becomes one of those viewers-with-alarm whose next step is the very hysteria of disorder they wish to escape. The hysteria of institutions is more dreadful than that of individuals.

R. P. Blackmur, *The Double agent*, quoted in
Literary Opinion in America, ed. Morton D. Zabel, p. 775n

1936

The editorial staff of the *Church Times* gnash their false teeth and quake in their galoshes at the mention of 'modern' (i.e. post-Tennysonian) poetry, but strange to say they make an exception of T. S. Eliot. Eliot is a declared Anglo-Catholic, and therefore his poetry, though 'modern', has got to be praised.

George Orwell, *Collected Essays* ... , I:290

Also I had lunch with Pope Eliot ... he *was* charming, a great man, I think, utterly unaffected ...

Dylan Thomas to Vernon Watkins, 20 April 1936

The Criterion under T. S. Eliot has been the best quarterly of our time.

Allen Tate, *Essays of Four Decades*, p. 54

Old Tom has issued all his poems in one vol, which he gives me. But theyre all known to you. Where he fails is when he takes on him to be a burly Englishman, with our gift for character drawing. Not a touch of Dickens or Shakespeare in him.

Virginia Woolf to Julian Bell, 2 May 1936

For our sins we only have a few pipers on hedges like Yeats and Tom Eliot, de la Mare—exquisite frail voices one has to hollow one's hand to hear, whereas old Wordsworth fills the room.

> Virginia Woolf to Ethel Smyth, 18 September 1936

Peter Lucas attacks Tom Eliot as usual, but he says for the last time.

> Virginia Woolf to Julian Bell, 14 November 1936

Eliot has produced his great effect upon his generation because he has described men and women that get out of bed or into it from mere habit; in describing this life that has lost heart his own art seems grey, cold, dry. He is an Alexander Pope, working without apparent imagination, producing his effects by a rejection of all rhythms and metaphors used by the more popular romantics rather than by the discovery of his own, this rejection giving his work an exaggerated plainness that has the effect of novelty. . . . I think of him as satirist rather than poet.

> W. B. Yeats, introduction to
> *Oxford Book of Modern Verse* (1936)

In the third year of the War [1917] came the most revolutionary man in poetry during my lifetime, though his revolution was stylistic alone—T. S. Eliot published his first book. No romantic word or sound, nothing reminiscent, . . . could be permitted henceforth. Poetry must resemble prose, and both must accept the vocabulary of their time; nor must there be any special subject-matter. . . . The past had deceived us: let us accept the worthless present. We older writers disliked this new poetry, but were forced to admit its satiric intensity.

> W. B. Yeats, "Modern Poetry,"
> *Yeats: Selected Criticism*, ed. Norman Jeffares, pp. 245–246

Eliot, the self-styled 'minor poet', brought back into English poetry the salt and the range of which it had long been deprived. From Dante through the Symbolists, he took what he needed from the varied stream of poetic resources; he swung the balance over from whimpering Georgian bucolics to forms wherein contemporary complexity could find expression. The *Collected Poems* are more than a work of poetic creation; they are a work of poetic regeneration.

Louise Bogan, *A Poet's Alphabet*, p. 108

I just wrote Eliot about you, hope it will do you some good. He seems to treat me very gingerly and cavalierly. He means to be warm-hearted, I suppose, but has grown such a crust that it is almost impossible.

Henry Miller to Lawrence Durrell, 6 December 1936

1937

You can cast them all in the shade, the [Edmund] Wilsons [T. S.] Eliots and Molly Columnists [Mary M. Colum]. I summon you to defend your country from the lot of them ...

Robert Frost to Louis Untermeyer, 24 December 1937

The rather limp versification of Mr. Eliot and of Mr. MacLeish is inseparable from the spiritual limpness that one feels behind the poems ...

Yvor Winters, *In Defense of Reason*, p. 22

... such national monuments as Havelock Ellis and T. S. Eliot ...

George Wickes, in *Lawrence Durrell and Henry Miller: A Private Correspondence*, p. 113

Tom Eliot is coming here next week end. I shall ask him, if I dare—but to ask him a question is like putting a penny in the slot of the Albert Hall—what he thinks about God.

Virginia Woolf to Ethel Smyth, 19 September 1937

Tom was miraculous at bowls, dignified, supple, regretted you, and showed up well . . . beside William Plomer.

Virginia Woolf to Angelica Bell, 2 October 1937

Tom Eliot was dining with us . . . Complete silence reigned. The poet ate; the novelist ate; Even Leonard, who had a chill inside, ate. Nothing of the least importance was said.

Virginia Woolf to V. Sackville-West, 26 December 1937

Old Tom . . . dined with us, but let on nothing; was in fact as genial and gentle as could be, and has mounted into the oddest world of antique respectability . . . I suppose in order to cultivate society dialogue for his play.

Virginia Woolf to Vanessa Bell, 28 December 1937

In praising this poem [by Margot Ruddock]'s feeling and restraint, the reviewer compared her work to the later poetry of T. S. Eliot, 'where only the restraint is present, the desire having been throttled before it was born', a judgment which seems likely to have been inspired by Yeats.

Roger McHugh, *Ah, Sweet Dancer:*
W. B. Yeats and Margot Ruddock, p. 132

Far from 'refuting' Eliot, his [Hart Crane's] whole career is a vindication of Eliot's major premise—that the integrity of the individual consciousness has broken down.

Allen Tate, *Essays of Four Decades*, p. 321

1938

Of all his literary heroes, none was the object of a more merciless array of fabricated anecdotes than T. S. Eliot, whose every secret Delmore pretended to know. . . . [But] Delmore was in fact astonishingly knowledgeable about Eliot's private life, and at a time when virtually nothing had been written about it.

James Atlas, *Delmore Schwartz*, pp. 118, 119n.

Today all writing is pretending to be Classical (Eliot, Heming-way, Stein) whereas the origins of it are really ROMANTIC. Compare *Waste Land* with Baudelaire ...

Lawrence Durrell to Henry Miller, August 1938

You have never sent me anything [for *The Listener*], excepting poor young men in need of work; do let me have something for this special number.

J. R. Ackerley to T. S. Eliot, 30 December 1938

1939

Eliot of late years has talked at great length about the value of religious experience. *The Family Reunion* is the first incontrovertible evidence that he has thoroughly experienced the phenomenon.

Louise Bogan, *A Poet's Alphabet*, p. 109

It devolved upon Eliot to become Delmore's model; he was, after all, the quintessential Modernist, and, what was perhaps more significant, he provided an example of the recognition conferred on those who managed to establish a new poetic idiom. And yet ... authoritarian, dignified, remote, Eliot had achieved a stature that infuriated Delmore even as it filled him with envy ...

James Atlas, *Delmore Schwartz*, p. 124

1940

It is possible that a man like T. S. Eliot illustrates the character [necessary to hold a chair of poetry], except that I regard him as a negative rather than a positive force.

Wallace Stevens to Henry Church, 15 October 1940

Eliot and I have our similarities and our differences. We are both poets and we both like to play. That's the similarity. The difference is this: I like to play euchre. He likes to play Eucharist.

Conversational remarks of Robert Frost, reported in
The Letters of Robert Frost to Louis Untermeyer, p. 321

Among the people who praised [Henry Miller's *Tropic of Cancer*] were T. S. Eliot, Herbert Read, Aldous Huxley, John Dos Passos, Ezra Pound—on the whole, not the writers who are in fashion at this moment....All of them are temperamentally hostile to the notion of 'progress'; it is felt that progress not only doesn't happen, but *ought not* to happen....Eliot's pessimism is partly the Christian pessimism, which implies a certain indifference to human misery, partly a lament over the decadence of western civilization..., a sort of twilight-of-the-gods feeling which finally leads him, in 'Sweeney Agonistes' for instance, to achieve the difficult feat of making modern life out to be worse than it is.

George Orwell, Collected Essays . . . , I:540, 556

1941

The characteristic writers of the nineteen-twenties—T. S. Eliot, for instance, Ezra Pound, Virginia Woolf—were writers who put the main emphasis on technique. They had their beliefs and prejudices, of course, but they were far more interested in technical innovations than in any moral or meaning or political implication that their work might contain.

George Orwell, Collected Essays . . . , II:150

1942

But what would Rudyard Kipling say—Had he lived to see this day—of having his poems edited by worlds-end-whimper T. S. Eliot . . . ?

Robert Frost to Lesley Frost Francis, 6 March 1942

There is very little in Eliot's later work that makes any deep impression on me.... I know a respectable quantity of Eliot's earlier work by heart.... It is clear that something has departed, some kind of current has been switched off, the later verse does not *contain* the earlier, even if it is claimed as an improvement upon it.... I do not know, but I should imagine that the struggle with meanings would have loomed smaller, and the poetry would have seemed to matter more, if he could have found his way to some creed which did not start off by forcing one to believe the incredible.

George Orwell, Collected Essays..., II:272, 273, 278

We usually arrange each number round a central theme and we think next time of having an American number. You are I think the only American poet at present in England, though there may be others, in which case I should be glad to hear about them. In any case we [the BBC] would like it very much if you would take part and read something of your own...

George Orwell to T. S. Eliot, 1942,
Collected Essays..., II:282

Pound and Eliot (like Picasso, Stravinsky, and Joyce) were in some sense expatriates in both space and time. They imported modernism into English rather more deliberately and openly than Wordsworth and Coleridge had imported romanticism...[and] while we were having the modernism of Pound, Stevens, Williams, Moore, Eliot, Tate, Crane, Cummings and all the rest, England was having the modernism of the Sitwells.

Randall Jarrell, The Nation, 21 February 1942

1943

T. S. Eliot is probably the most widely respected literary figure of our time; he is known primarily as the leader of the intellectual reaction against the romanticism of which he began his career as a disciple. It is my purpose to show that his intellectualism and his reactionary position are alike an illusion.

Yvor Winters, In Defense of Reason, p. 460

Some things that the Norton Chair [of Poetry] has done have been to the good: for instance, it brought Eliot over and had him live in Cambridge [Mass.] for a few months.

Wallace Stevens to Henry Church, 30 March 1943

If you ask a 'good party man' (and this goes for almost any party of the Left) what he objects to in Eliot, you get an answer that ultimately reduces to this. Eliot is a reactionary (he has declared himself a royalist, an Anglo-Catholic, etc.), and he is also a 'bourgeois intellectual', out of touch with the common man: therefore he is a bad writer. Contained in this statement is a half-conscious confusion of ideas which vitiates nearly all politico-literary criticism.

George Orwell, Collected Essays . . . , II:335

Eliot underestimated his 'lower classes'. . . . The various mechanical devices which Eliot feared and deplored have served, as a matter of fact, to aid the development and dissemination of this folk art.

Louise Bogan, A Poet's Alphabet, p. 140

1944

That Eliot found what I thought his needlessly lost soul in the socially powerful but intellectually negligible Anglican Church did nothing to incline me to take his verse more seriously.

Frederic J. Osborn to Lewis Mumford, 19 June 1944

Read *The Rock*, by T. S. Eliot, with great admiration, particularly the first page and its masterly statements on our ignorance. And these questions: 'Where is the wisdom we lost in knowledge? Where is the knowledge we lost in information?' One would like to see such lines inscribed on the fronton [pediment] of every university in the world.

Julian Green, Diary, 1928–1957, p. 142

Witness the renewed highbrow-baiting that is now going on in this country and America, with its outcry not only against Joyce, Proust and Lawrence, but even against T. S. Eliot.

George Orwell, *Collected Essays . . .* , III:189

Exceptions can, of course, be found, but it is broadly true that anyone who would prefer T. S. Eliot to Alfred Noyes despises England, or thinks that he ought to do so.

George Orwell, *Collected Essays . . .* , III:53–54

Without even getting up from this table to consult a book I can think of passages in . . . T. S. Eliot and many another which would be called antisemitic if they had been written since Hitler came to power.

George Orwell, *Collected Essays . . .* , III:113

Now Eliot, as it happens, is one of the few writers of our time who have tried seriously to write English as it is spoken.

George Orwell, *Collected Essays . . .* , III:164

Eliot has been working for the British Council for a couple of years. . . . To judge by his private conversation he has definitely changed some of his political views, though he hasn't made any public pronouncement yet.

George Orwell to Rayner Heppenstall, 17 July 1944,
Collected Essays . . . , III:218

My only consolation now is Lao-tse of which Eliot kindly sent me a copy—funny patient crazy rectangular man that he is.

Lawrence Durrell to Henry Miller, 23 May 1944

[*Four Quartets* is] a quasi-autobiographical experience of the *union with God*, or rather its imperfect approximation in this life.

Robert Lowell, quoted in Steven Gould Axelrod,
Robert Lowell: Life and Art, pp. 46–47.

1945

Eliot can dramatize his lyrics but rarely projects dramatic action with force.... Eliot's importance is based on the fact that he had the sensitiveness and the melancholy foreboding to sense the general tragedy of his period when that tragedy had not yet impressed other observers.... How gloomy everyone was, after Eliot!

Louise Bogan, *A Poet's Alphabet*, p. 41

Hattie Flanagan [theatrical director] proposed putting me on somewhere even as she had put on Eliot and Auden but I said Whizz I had rather she thought of me in connection with [Oscar] Wilde than with them two.

Robert Frost to Louis Untermeyer, 18 July 1945

1946

Eliot is not only the most important poet writing in English but also a distinguished essayist, critic and lecturer ... Life, for him, is not pleasure; indeed, for Eliot pleasure has something in it of sarcasm; it gives the impression of a bruised fruit, a wound in a tender body. For him the element which makes mankind alive is the struggle between good and evil.... He is a rare example of a poet who feels, thinks, struggled with himself, and develops a self-disciplined, almost mystical devotion to his work.

George Seferis, *On the Greek Style*, pp. 124, 154, 155

Eliot—tradition is too organized with him, his uncertainty before chaos leads him to confuse authority with orthodoxy ...

Charles Olson, *Human Universe*, p. 99

If Eliot and other contemporary poets have any characteristic fault, it may be in planning too much.

W. K. Wimsatt, *The Verbal Icon*, p. 17

...lunched at the Holland Park to see T. S. Eliot's new play *Family Reunion*. It approached parody at moments but the audience was devout. The programme said it was the story of Agamemnon. Except for a Greek sense of doom and a Greek technique in the use of choruses there was no connection apparent to me. The main fault was that it aroused too much intellectual curiosity about the details of the plot. I think a story must be well known before it can be treated in that way.

Evelyn Waugh, *Diaries*, p. 666

1947

I saw Eliot—gentle, sweet, now older, more grey and worn-looking, but very gentle and tired. He gives off a radiance now I didn't notice before—always felt he was like a senior civil servant.

Lawrence Durrell to Henry Miller, June 1947

I found your friend [T. S. Eliot] wearied (as was natural) & kindly (as is surprising)

E. E. Cummings to Ezra Pound, 27 May 1947

Per contra (alias entr' ourselves) a not unrecent peep at Tears Eliot... has mightily confirmed my negligible suspicion that be it never so humble there's no: Solly, after entertaining that hombre for 15 minutes you feel like taking out a patent for manipulating the dead

E. E. Cummings to Sir Solly Zuckerman, 1 June 1947

I'm glad Tom Eliot was well, when you saw him. He is a man for whom I have always had a great affection, (though I have never been very intimate with him, in spite of nearly thirty years of acquaintance) as well as a profound admiration.

Aldous Huxley to E. McKnight Kauffer,
19 January 1947

T. S. Eliot broadcast his *Four Quartets* here last night in good voice and with the exact rhythm in which I read them in print, and I envied his advantage in being able to dodge all the difficult stages in his argument, and thereby to seem much more profound than he is. Mind you, I think a poet is entitled to dodge in this way when he is seized with some idea on the very margin of the capacity of the human mind. Eliot's effects remind me of a cotton wool snowstorm in a children's pantomime, where the management will not allow the property man enough cotton wool to last out the scene.

Frederic J. Osborn to Lewis Mumford,
6 September 1947

Mr. Eliot, I think, has been trying for a solution of this problem of perspective in his recent verse. *The Waste Land* gave us violent juxtapositions of images at different levels of intensity, and of image with deliberately banal or flashing statement. But in *Four Quartets* the transitions are much less abrupt...

C. Day Lewis, *The Poetic Image*, p. 95

1948/1952

These were the years just before the great catastrophe to our letters—the appearance of T. S. Eliot's *The Waste Land*.... Our work staggered to a halt for a moment under the blast of Eliot's genius which gave the poem back to the academics. We did not know how to answer him.... This is not to say that Eliot has not, indirectly, contributed much to the emergence of the next step in metrical construction, but if he had not turned away from the direct attack here,... we might have gone ahead much faster.... To have the man run out that way drove me mad. I have never quite got over it...

William Carlos Williams, *Autobiography*, pp. 146, 175.

1948

...the distinguished poet and literary arbiter T. S. Eliot...

W. K. Wimsatt, *The Verbal Icon*, p. 85

It is nonsense what Fyvel said about Eliot being anti-semitic. Of course you can find what would now be called antisemitic remarks in his early work, but who didn't say such things at that time? One has to draw a distinction between what was said before and what after 1934.... In the early twenties, Eliot's antisemitic remarks were about on a par with the automatic sneer one casts at Anglo-Indian colonels in boarding houses.

George Orwell to Julian Symons,
29 October 1948,
Collected Essays ..., IV:509

Probably, ... Mr. Eliot does not believe in class distinctions as our grandfathers believed in them. His approval of them is only negative. That is to say, he cannot see how any civilization worth having can survive in a society where the differences arising from social background or geographical origin have been ironed out.... A genuinely classless society ... Mr. Eliot assumes would be a cultureless society. He may be right, but at some points his pessimism seems to be exaggerated.

George Orwell, *Collected Essays* ..., IV:516–517

1948 [?]

Mr. Eliot ... is a very subtle creator—who knows how to squeeze the last ounce of force out of his material. He has done a good job here [*Four Quartets*] though when he speaks of developing a new manner of writing, new manners following new manners only to be spent as soon as that particular piece of writing has been accomplished—I do not think he quite knows what he is about. But in spite of everything and completely discounting his subject matter, his *genre*, Eliot's experiments in the *Quartets* show him to be more American in the sense I seek than ... Auden ... will ever be able to be.

William Carlos Williams, quoted in
American Poetic Theory,
ed. George Perkins, pp. 250–251.

Mr. Eliot's early theory I should call advanced romantic criticism: it was struggling through the subjective effect towards the objective structure of the work. Longinus' criticism of Sappho is advanced romantic criticism, as advanced as Mr. Eliot's.

Allen Tate, *Essays of Four Decades*, pp. 483–484

In recent years Yeats and Eliot have used the recurrent symbol with great effect. Eliot has risked a great deal more on it than Yeats.

E. M. W. Tillyard, *Poetry Direct and Oblique*, p. 66

I had never hoped to see the greatest poet of our time properly honoured and reverenced [by the order of Merit]. Well, I have.

Edith Sitwell to T. S. Eliot, 1 January 1948

1949

[Bowra] brings out two virtues often overlooked in Eliot—his exquisite ear, and his insistence upon dramatic balance as well as intellectual content.

Louise Bogan, *A Poet's Alphabet*, p. 68

When we think of the character of literary dictators in the past, it is easy to see that since 1922 Eliot has occupied a position in the English-speaking world analogous to that occupied by Ben Jonson, Dryden, Pope, Samuel Johnson, Coleridge, and Matthew Arnold.... Throughout Eliot's criticism the quality of the poet's language and its effect upon the future of the English language has always concerned Eliot very much. I think we can say that never before has criticism been so conscious of all that can happen to language, how easily it can be debased, and how marvelously it can be elevated and made to illuminate the most difficult and delicate areas of experience.

Delmore Schwartz, "The Literary Dictatorship of T. S. Eliot," *Partisan Review*, February 1949

Eliot may still be our best critic because his constant frames of reference are large and loose, the frame of the particular essay being improvised, tentative and variable; he does not board the juggernaut of methodology and he heeps the faith (by and large) with the work that he is presumably examining.

Allen Tate, *Essays of Four Decades*, p. 170

All the best critics of Pound's work . . . have been blinded, perhaps, by the notion of the 'impersonality' of the poet. This perverse and valuable doctrine . . . [is] associated in our time with Eliot's name . . .

John Berryman,
The Freedom of the Poet, p. 264

the latest biglimag of-by-&-for uncle tom's [T. S. Eliot's] lapdogs complacently avers (page blank-319) that their Master's Voice occupies a complete 'album' of 'five 12-inch records' . . .

E. E. Cummings to Allen Tate, 9 July 1949

He [Charles Williams]'s quite unreadable . . . I think Eliot's approval of him must be purely sectarian (Anglo-Catholic). It wouln't surprise me to learn that Eliot approves of C. S. Lewis as well. The more I see the more I doubt whether people ever really make aesthetic judgments at all. Everything is judged on political grounds which are then given an aesthetic disguise.

George Orwell
to Richard Rees, 28 July 1949,
Collected Essays . . ., IV:567

1950

Yeats and Pound achieved modernity; Eliot was modern from the start.

Louise Bogan, *A Poet's Alphabet*, p. 11

Mr Eliot has become a public institution, a part of the establishment.... [but] Mr Eliot is a much greater and more significant poet than his Anglo-Catholic admirers make him.... Eliot's genius is that of the great poet who has a profound and acute apprehension of the difficulties of his age.

> F. R. Leavis, "Retrospect 1950,"
> in *New Bearings in English Poetry*, pp. 177, 180, 181

I was discouraged by reading The Cocktail Party...What a meager and spiritless work.

> John Dos Passos to Edmund Wilson, 19 July 1950

Shall we say that Eliot, in his determination to put poetic drama honestly within reach of an audience, has uttered a thinner and plainer version of the themes and images of his major and more densely implicated poems? To say so need not, I believe, be a disparagement.... There are poetic virtues of chasteness, restraint, terseness precision. These are the presiding virtues of Eliot's comedy [*The Cocktail Party*].

> W. K. Wimsatt, *Hateful Contraries*, p. 189

As a matter of fact, I don't know him [T. S. Eliot] at all and have had no correspondence whatever with him.... All I knew about him in the days of Others was the correspondence between him and the people who were running Others. After all, Eliot and I are dead opposites and I have been doing about everything that he would not be likely to do.

> Wallace Stevens to William Van O'Connor,
> 25 April 1950

1951

Gabriela [Mistral] described Eliot as 'un hombre muy tímido.' [an exceedingly timid man]

> Quoted in Carlos Baker, *Ernest Hemingway*, p. 496

You think I am wrong about Eliot. There is too much of the well-fed votary of Helicon in him, and real seers are waifs, or Ishmaels waiting for the angelic waters to spring up in the wilderness. Maybe what is wrong is that he no longer has to wait. It is a terrible evil to have everything.

Edward Dahlberg to Herbert Read,
15 November 1951

So far have the more influential critics of our time been from practicing a style of neutral explication (and I think here not only of Eliot but especially of Leavis and Pound) that it would be nearer to the truth to say that they have mainly depended on two nonexplicative powers: a confident good taste in pointing out passages and quoting them and an energetic, authoritarian bent for exhortation—that is, telling us we ought to admire these passages.

W. K. Wimsatt,
The Verbal Icon, p. 247

1952

I was talking to an English poet the other day and, as Eliot's name was mentioned, I said that I was very fond of the poet, without being very sensitive to the music of his verse, even in *Four Quartets*, and doubted if there were any. 'Yes, there is,' he replied gently, 'but it is everyday music'.

Julian Green,
Diary, 1928–1957, p. 251

I regard T. S. Eliot's poems as evil ...

Edward Dahlberg to Herbert Read,
19 January 1952

1953

It was the introduction of a sense of rhythms foreign to classic English, in three English-speaking 'foreigners', that finally broke the iambic hold. These poets—William Butler Yeats, Ezra Pound, and T. S. Eliot—by their experiments changed the iambic line so that it again became flexible and vigorous.... Eliot himself...[is] one of the greatest English metrists...

> Louise Bogan, *A Poet's Alphabet*, pp. 156–157

1954

You know I have a niggard respect for Eliot's poems...Eliot's *Quartet*...I regard as mediocre.

> Edward Dahlberg to Herbert Read, 13 January 1954

I am not conscious of having been influenced by anybody and have purposely held off from reading highly mannered people like Eliot and Pound so that I should not absorb anything, even unconsciously.

> Wallace Stevens to Richard Eberhart, 15 January 1954

1955

Eliot is a wild son of Ham, and he will not last; when his books are chaff in the wind you will have pensive readers. The evil he is is in the rabble titles of his volumes, *Murder in the Cathedral* and *The Cocktail Party*, which are a claim for cash.

> Edward Dahlberg to Herbert Read, 1 March 1955

As Dante's rose is his preface to illumination so, for many of us today, T. S. Eliot is the preface to Dante and to such illumination as we enjoy.

> William York Tindall, *The Literary Symbol*, p. 29

1956–1962

Eliot's *Waste Land* may have been during the 1920's, to persons of a settled religious thought and habit, a somewhat shocking poem.

W. K. Wimsatt, *Hateful Contraries*, p. 45

1957

Eliot is at times inconsistent, but he seems never to subscribe seriously to the notion that the poet's main job is to hand over to the reader some determinate content, whether an emotion or an idea, or that the poet's effectiveness is to measured by the success of this transaction. On the contrary, the weight of Eliot's prestige has been thrown behind a quite antithetical conception: an anti-Romantic, 'impersonal' art, in which the claims of the art object, with all their complexity and indeterminacy have first consideration.

W. K. Wimsatt and Cleanth Brooks,
Literary Criticism, p. 669

1958

Old TSE was a masterly critic and a very helpful publisher. Any poetic reputation I have is due to his persuasion—to cut out dud poems, verbose ones, poems bulging with connective tissue. I often thought him wrong and attacked; but patiently, wisely, he really did convince me.

Lawrence Durrell to Henry Miller, October 1958

Tom Eliot...is now curiously dull—as a result, perhaps, of being, at last, happy in his second marriage...

Aldous Huxley to Humphry Osmond,
16 December 1958

He [E. M. Forster] is a far greater man than T. S. Eliot, and if he came to your house you would never say about him, when you ushered him out, as you said about Eliot 'It was like entertaining royalty'. And you would have had a much more interesting evening, to boot.

J. R. Ackerley to Stephen Spender, 26 November 1958

1959

It is probably not until about the time of Mr. Eliot and his friends that the free and subtle moving in and out and coalescing of strong-stress and syllable-stress meters in the same poem, the same stanza, begins to appear with any frequency. This is something remarkable in the history of metrics.

W. K. Wimsatt, *Hateful Contraries*, p. 145

1960

"Like a patient etherised upon a table . . . " With this line, modern poetry begins.

John Berryman, *The Freedom of the Poet*, p. 270

Last night at Eliot's was magnificcnt. . . . I felt to be sitting next to a descended god; he has such a nimbus of greatness about him. . . . Wonderfully wry and humorous.

Sylvia Plath to Aurelia S. Plath, 5 May 1960

Eliot errs a little less blatantly [than Pound] because he is a colder sharper; but none of these men have the least amount of blood circulating through their verse or prose. The salt marshes near Cadiz taste sweeter than their technical rot.

Edward Dahlberg to Josephine Herbst, 16 May 1960

1961

T. S. Eliot has done a good deal to expose the superficialities accompanying the popularization of liberal ideas, but he has done so by attacking habits of feeling rather than ideas as such.... [Eliot's] weakness for attitudes he might honestly mean, but had not honestly come by, became more marked [after the 1920s]...That Eliot can be callow when away from literature is no news, but he has never before shown himself so callow, or even silly, as here [in *Notes towards the Definition of Culture*].

Clement Greenberg, Art and Culture, p. 22

It is not very sensible to throw away Wycherley, Will Congreve, Dryden, Etherege, while you espouse the small, brittle puns, and the scatological jokes of Pound and Eliot.

Edward Dahlberg to Stanley Burnshaw, 1 November 1961

1962 [?]

Americans like Eliot...could be as curious about French or Italian poetry as about English and could hear poetry of the past, like the verse of Webster, freshly in a way that for an Englishman, trammeled by traditional notions of Elizabethan blank verse, would have been difficult.

W. H. Auden, The Dyer's Hand, p. 367

1962

Eliot even sinks in a line that is good in another poet.... A truth in the mouth of Pontius Pilate is always a lie.

Edward Dahlberg to Stanley Burnshaw,
27 January 1962

[Roethke] attacked Eliot's bloodless pedantry...
Allan Seager, *The Glass House:
The Life of Theodore Roethke*, p. 280

1963

One of the very few good things Eliot ever said was that Europeans study a writer as a whole, whereas the American is concerned with fragments, or to repeat, the last book—and there has always got to be a last new book or else the author is as good as dead.

Edward Dahlberg to Josephine Herbst, 2 November 1963

...the intellectualism represented by men like Eliot, Ransom, and Winters has seen order as exclusively intellectual order...

Allen Tate, *Essays of Four Decades*, p. 379

1964

...some way along the table T. S. Eliot, a wizened little man leaning over his plate and gazing fixedly at it and listening to the speeches with a rare indulgence in a half-smile.

Frederic J. Osborn to Lewis Mumford, 27 May 1964

A large body of Anglo-American verse has indeed been influenced by the revolution which Eliot brought about, and one could find throughout the poetry of such men as MacLeish, Auden, Jarrell, and Warren plenty of instances of this strain of witty, intellectual verse, which makes emphatic use of the verbal medium, including complicated metaphor and involved symbolism. But pervasive as the influence of Eliot has been, it has not been the sole modern influence, and the tide that turned against it some years ago is now at full flood.

Cleanth Brooks, *A Shaping Joy*, p. 54

1965

The death of [Stan] Laurel saddened me more than the deaths of Edith [Sitwell], Eliot, or Churchill.

J. R. Ackerley to Geoffrey Gorer, 27 February 1965

How can one deal adequately with an influence so powerful and pervasive as that which T. S. Eliot has exerted upon the last half-century? Truly one is confronted with an embarrassment of riches: the poet, the dramatist, the critic, the editor, the student of culture—all invite attention, and two of Eliot's roles, those of poet and critic, demand it.

Cleanth Brooks, A Shaping Joy, p. 37

1966

As he grew older Eliot was never fanatical about his literary ideas and opinions, and he mixed grace with courage in retracting quite a few of them, as on the subject of Milton, for instance; nor did he ever lose sight of the literary object in expounding his religious convictions. . . . Thus Eliot persuades us once again that he is the finest literary critic of this century in the English language. His only possible rival is Edmund Wilson. . . . Eliot is dead and we will not soon see his like again. He was one of the principal educators of the imaginative life of his age, a uniquely great shaping influence both as poet and critic.

Phillip Rahv, Essays on Literature and Politics,
pp. 78–79, 82, 84

1967

In writing his verse plays, Mr. Eliot took, I believe, the only possible line. Except at a few unusual moments, he kept the style Drab.

W. H. Auden, Secondary Worlds, p. 116

1968

I got his [Eliot's] *Poems* (1920)...and I couldn't write anything
for several months. This man, though by no means famous at
that time, was evidently so thoroughly my contemporary that I
had been influenced by him before I had read a line of his verse.
There were two great poems in that volume that seemed to do
everything that I wanted to do...I thought I had better do
something else than become a writer...

Allen Tate, *Essays
of Four Decades*, pp. 225–226

...a poet-critic who did as much as any other single authority
to establish in English studies of the mid-century a climate
favorable to objective inquiry—T. S. Eliot, of course.

W. K. Wimsatt,
Day of the Leopards, p. 14

A sophisticated version of Pater's *Renaissance*, adjusted to an
anti-Victorian view of English literary history, made its
appearance in T. S. Eliot...

F. W. Bateson,
A Guide to English Literature, p. 44

1969

Eliot was a decisive influence on taste and critical fashion....I
see Eliot's creative career as a sustained, heroic and indefatiga-
bly resourceful quest of a profound sincerity of the most difficult kind. The heroism is that of genius.

F. R. and Q. D. Leavis,
Lectures in America, p. 30

1971

Eliot is deficient on a formal level; that's why he talks about form. Pound actually rewrote "The Wasteland" and that's why it has the form it has. Eliot does not understand total form.... Eliot has to imitate form.... This is Eliot's weakness.

Robert Duncan, in *Allen Verbatim*,
ed. Gordon Hall, p. 108

Part III

Ezra Pound

Ezra Pound:
A Brief Chronology

1885	Born on 30 October in Hailey, Idaho
1889	Family moves to Philadelphia, where Homer Pound, his father, works in U.S. Mint
1891–1901	Attends private schools
1898	First trip to Europe
1901–1903	Attends University of Pennsylvania; meets William Carlos Williams
1903–1905	Transfers to Hamilton College; completes B.A.
1905–1906	Graduate work in comparative literature at University of Pennsylvania; meets Hilda Doolittle [H. D.], to whom he is engaged; completes M.A.
1906	Awarded travelling fellowship, spends summer in Europe
1907	Graduate work continues; teaching post at Wabash College
1907–1908	Resigns teaching post under fire; travels to Venice, there publishes *A Lume Spento*; travels to London, there publishes *A Quinzaine for This Yule*
1909	Publishes *Personae* and *Exultations*
1910	Publishes *The Spirit of Romance*; visits Europe and U.S.

1912	Publishes *Ripostes*; begins work with Harriet Monroe and *Poetry*
1914	Marries Dorothy Shakespear; meets T. S. Eliot; *Blast* begins publication
1915	Publishes *Cathay*
1916	Publishes *Lustra* and *Gaudier-Brzeska*
1917	Publishes *Noh* ...
1918	Publishes *Pavannes and Divisions*
1920	Publishes *Instigations, Mauberley, Umbra*, and *Homage to Sextus Propertius*; leaves London for Paris
1924	Settles in Rapallo, Italy
1925	Publishes *A Draft of XVI Cantos*
1926	Publishes *Personae* [Collected shorter poems]
1930	Publishes *A Draft of XXX Cantos*
1931	Publishes *How to Read*
1932	Publishes *Guido Cavalcanti* ...
1933	Publishes *ABC of Economics*; has interview with Mussolini
1934	Publishes *Make It New* and *ABC of Reading*; meets James Laughlin
1935	Publishes *Jefferson and/or Mussolini*
1937	Publishes *The Fifth Decad of Cantos*
1938	Publishes *Guide to Kulchur*
1939	Visits U.S.
1940	Publishes *Cantos LII-LXXI*
1941–1943	Broadcasts over Radio Rome
1945	Arrested, jailed at Pisa, indicted for treason, remanded to mental hospital, St. Elizabeth's, in Washington, D.C.
1948–1949	Publishes *The Pisan Cantos*; awarded Bollingen Prize
1950	*The Letters of Ezra Pound* is published
1954	Publishes *The Classic Anthology Defined by Confucius*; T. S. Eliot edits *Literary Essays of Ezra Pound*

1955	Publishes *Rock-Drill de Los Cantares*
1958	Released from St. Elizabeth's, returns to Italy
1959	Publishes *Thrones de los Cantares*
1965	Visits England, for T. S. Eliot's funeral
1969	Visits U.S.
1972	Dies on 1 November

1892

Even at the age of six he was so seized with indignation at the result of a national election that he hurled his rocking-chair across the room.

Noel Stock, *The Life of Ezra Pound*, p. 7

1900–1904

Ezra Pound was writing a daily sonnet. He destroyed them all at the end of the year; I never saw any of them.... [He] would come to my room to read me his poems, the very early ones, some of those in *A Lume Spento*. It was a painful experience.... Ezra never explained or joked about his writing as I might have done, but was always cryptic, unwavering and serious...He joked, crudely, about anything but that....He was the livest, most intelligent and most unexplainable thing I'd ever seen, and the most fun...He was often brilliant but an ass....And he had, at bottom, an inexhaustible patience, an infinite depth of human imagination and sympathy. Vicious, catty at times, neglectful, if he trusted you not to mind, but warm and devoted...

William Carlos Williams,
Autobiography, pp. 56–58

Pound...is a fine fellow; he is the essence of optimism and has a cast-iron faith...If he ever does get blue nobody knows it...But not one person in a thousand likes him, and a great many people detest him and why? Because he is so darned full of conceits and affectation.... It is too bad, for he loves to be liked, yet there is some quality in him which makes him too proud to try to please people.... He is afraid of being taken in if he trusts his really tender heart to the mercies of a cruel crowd and so keeps it hidden and trusts no one.

William Carlos Williams
to his mother, 30 March 1904

Immensely sophisticated, immensely superior, immensely rough-and-ready, a product not like any of the . . . boys we danced with (and he danced badly). One would dance with him for what he might say. They would say, "He is so eccentric. . . . He is impossible; he told Professor Schelling that Bernard Shaw was more important than Shakespeare. . . . He makes himself conspicuous; he wore lurid, bright socks that the older students ruled out for freshmen. The sophomores threw him in the lily pond. They called him 'Lily' Pound."

H. D. [Hilda Doolittle], End to Torment, pp. 3, 14

1906

Mad? He always was eccentric. "O, Ezra Pound's crazy," was the verdict of my schoolgirl contemporaries.

H. D., End of Torment, p. 20

1907

It was Ezra who really introduced me to William Morris. He literally shouted "The Gilliflower of Gold" in the orchard. . . . He was a composite James McNeill Whistler, Peer Gynt and the victorious and defeated heroes of the William Morris poems and stories. He read me "The Haystack in the Floods" with passionate emotion. . . . He called me Is-hilda and wrote a sonnet a day; he bound them in a parchment folder.

H. D. End of Torment, pp. 22–23.

At Crawfordsville [site of Wabash College] he came across that atmosphere of dislike met several times before. A colleague considered that there was much of the showman and the charlatan about him then—a superficially brilliant and interesting man. For the [college] authorities he was to prove "too much the Latin Quarter type."

Patricia Hutchins, Ezra Pound's Kensington, p. 39

He seemed unintimidated by the fact that (to my mind) he had no ear for music and, alas, I suffered excruciatingly from his clumsy dancing. I suffered, indeed I suppose we all did. He himself, in a certain sense, made no mistakes. He gave, he took. He gave extravagantly.

H. D. End of Torment, p. 49

Miss Adele Polk...remembered one day at the Pound home when Ezra, using a sideboard or buffet for a chair, methodically pulled out the tail of his shirt as he talked, carefully tore off a square of material, with gravity placed the square on his knee, and tapped it during the rest of the conversation. She could not fathom his purpose but she was impressed.

Noel Stock, The Life of Ezra Pound, pp. 25–26

Fred H. Rhodes who was a member of one of Pound's French classes [at Wabash College] described him as "exhibitionistic, egotistic, self-centered, and self-indulgent."

Noel Stock, The Life of Ezra Pound, p. 42

"I remember Pound then," [F. S.] Flint laughed. "He had a tuppeny ha'penny sort of room, the bed taking up most of the space, beside it a *ruelle* [space between bed and wall] in which he received his visitors. Ezra used to sit on the bed and recite Arnaut Daniel, which sounded like Bantu clicks." At one time Flint saw a very fine copy of Tacitus in Pound's room and asked if he could read it, and Pound replied, "I hope so!"

Quoted from Patricia Hutchins,
Ezra Pound's Kensington, p. 56

[*A Lume Spento* contains] wild haunting stuff, absolutely poetic, original, imaginative, passionate and spiritual. Those who do not consider it crazy may well consider it inspired. Coming after the trite and decorous verse of most of our decorous poets, this poet seems like a minstrel of Provence at a suburban musical evening.

Review, unsigned,
in The Evening Standard (London), 1908

Success to you, young singer in Venice! Success to "With Tapers Quenched [*A Lume Spento*]."

Ella Wheeler Wilcox, in *The New York American-Journal-Examiner*, 14 December 1908

1909

Mr. Pound is talented, but he is very young. The academician bristles all over his work . . . and the carelessness that attends the swift birth of an idea is all over his work. He affects obscurity and loves the abstruse.

Review of *A Lume Spento*, unsigned, in *Books News Monthly*, May 1909

His aim was less to promote Ezra Pound than to propagate new standards for verse. . . . Yeats . . . dominated the dinner table [at a literary dinner] . . . and Pound, either bored with hearing his [own] views at second hand or eager to draw some attention to himself, took one of the tulips decorating the table and munched it, petal by petal. . . . Pound then went on to eat the remainder of the tulips—a Noble-Savage-from-America performance he would repeat at other houses and among other guests.

Stanley Weintraub, *The London Yankees*, pp. 265, 266

Mr. Pound has any amount of affectations, and sometimes is incoherent in order to seem original, but, in spite of drawbacks, he manages to suggest his essential sincerity. It is a queer little book which will irritate many readers. We dislike its faults, and . . . yet we are attracted occasionally by lines which are almost, if not quite, nonsense. Our conclusion is that Mr. Pound is a poet, though a fantastic one.

Review of *Personae*, unsigned, in *The Evening Standard and St. James's Gazette*, 16 April 1909

Here is a poet with individuality and with sufficient disregarding for the conventional to express that individuality in the way that likes him best rather than in the way which more accomodating talents would have chosen.... There is through all a thread of true beauty, which gives the book [*Personae*] something of a haunting charm.... Mr. Pound is of the few who hve gone forth into life and found something of a new seed, and his "flower" is one that is unquestionably beautiful, though it will scarcely please many of those who prefer rather new varieties of the old favourites.

W. L. Courtney, in
The Daily Telegraph, 23 April 1909

Again we have the spectacle of a really sincere and vigorous artist driven by his revolt against the abuse of law and convention into mere chaos.... We can find nothing but evidence of a highly interesting personality unable to express itself.

Review of *Exultations*, unsigned, in
The Birmingham Daily Post, 1909, as cited
by Stock, *The Life of Ezra Pound*, p. 75.

This writer has in him the capacity for remarkable poetic achievement, but ... at present he is somewhat weighted by his learning. His virility and passion are immense, but ... he strikes us a little too bookish and literary, even when he is most untrammelled by metrical conventions. It is ungracious to carp at work which in itself is so fine, but we think it right to hint at the danger.

Review of *Exultations*, unsigned,
in *The Spectator*, 11 December 1909

Crowned with a mass of bright fair hair and often bearded; wearing a velvet coat and one turquoise ear-ring...I always saw him, not so much as a poet, as the warrior of the arts and the vigour and enthusiasm with which he waged his battles against the pudwiggens of the academic and literary traditions were as valuable as they were immense.

Edgar Jepson, *Memories of
an Edwardian*, p. 152

Here is Ezra Pound & I think he has very great things in him & the love poems . . . —in fact nearly all—are extraordinary achievements. . . . Ezra Pound's second book was a miserable thing & I was guilty of a savage recantation after meeting the man at dinner. It was very treacherous & my severity was due to self-contempt as much as dislike of his work.

Edward Thomas to Gordon Bottomley,
1 May and 14 December 1909

It is easier to enjoy than to praise Mr. Pound, easier to find fault with him, easiest to ridicule.

Edward Thomas, in *The English Review*, June 1909

Ezra Pound . . . is a well-known American poet—a good one. He is 24, like me, but his god is beauty, mine life.

D. H. Lawrence to Louis Burrows, November 1909

Ezra Pound . . . has I think got closer to the right sort of music for poetry than Mrs. Emery [Florence Farr]—it is more definitely music with strongly marked time and yet it is effective speech.

W. B. Yeats to Lady Gregory, 10 December 1909

Mr Pound is a poet with a distinct personality. Essentially, he is a rebel against all conventions except sanity; there is something robustly impish and elfish about him. . . . This book [*Personae*] is as tufted with beauty as the bole of an old elm tree with green shoots.

F. S. Flint, in *The New Age*, 27 May 1909

His virtues and faults are both obvious. He is blatant, full of foolish archaisms, obscure through awkward language not subtle thought, and formless; he tastes experience keenly, has an individual outlook, flashes into brilliance, occasionally, and expresses roughly a good deal of joy in life. . . . Mr. Pound has great talents. When he has passed through stammering to speech, and when he has more clearly recognized the nature of poetry, he may be a great poet.

Rupert Brooke, in *The Cambridge Review*,
2 December 1909

Mr Welkin Mark . . . begs to announce that he has secured for the English market the palpitating works of the new Montana (U.S.A.) poet, Mr. Ezekiel Tom, who is the most remarkable thing in poetry since Robert Browning.

Punch, 23 June 1909

Pound is said to have read ["Sestina: Altaforte"] so forcefully at a poets' dinner arranged by [T. E.] Hulme at the Tour Eiffel restaurant in Percy Street in 1909 that the management placed a screen round their table.

Noel Stock, *The Life of Ezra Pound*, p. 69

One is glad to welcome another tiny volume of most delicate verse from Mr. Ezra Pound, whose *Personae* had a charm of fancy and of finish that has carried it to a high degree of success.

Review of *Exultations*, unsigned, in *The Observer*, 26 December 1909

There is in Mr. Pound's new book [*Exultations*] a rift of real, though vague, beauty, impalpable gold . . .

F. S. Flint, in *The New Age*, 6 January 1910

At first the books [*Personae* and *Exultations*] seem to be an imbroglio of egotistical nonsense, but gradually we are able to discern the arcs of out-running laws . . . His style . . . is often involved, obscure, and pedantic, and there is a certain disagreeable insistence upon the value of the poetic rind itself. But on the other hand the lines are almost oppressive with their unexpanded power, with their intensity and passion, and they are full to the fingertips with an extremely interesting personality. Mr. Pound has given the vessel of poetry a rather violent shaking, but we are thankful to him for it, even though many dregs should be brought to the surface.

Review, unsigned, in *The Literary Digest*, 26 February 1910

He [Pound] feels, as many others feel, that the range of vocabulary in English poetry might advantageously be widened.

Darrell Figgis, in *The New Age*, 1910

Mr. Pound's two little books [*Personae* and *Exultations*] ... might almost be used as touch-stones for the finding of what is genuine in the poetry of our time.... Mr. Pound is obedient to some instinctive harmony, which, if one will lay aside prejudice and dance to his piping, creates for us a new world of transfigured sound and colour.

Griffith Fairfax, in *The Melbourne Book Lover*, 6 April 1910

Leaning uncomfortably against a tall window was a young man with a large hat cocked over one eye, introduced by the editor [of *The New Age*] as Ezra Pound.... My outstanding first impression was of a highly-strung, extremely mercurial personality ... In some way there was an uncommonly elegant look about the young newcomer.

Arthur Thorn, quoted from Patricia Hutchins, *Ezra Pound's Kensington*, p. 108

Not since the death of Whistler had London seen and heard an American who dared to storm the fortresses of aesthetic opinion with so much ease and wit.... He was less tactful than irresistible—and as a critic and teacher, less pedantic than highhanded and spirited.... Like a knight-errant he pricked and exploded inflated literary reputations and fought the standards of merely "popular taste," as well as the accepted values of middle-class, middle-brow culture.

Horace Gregory, *Amy Lowell*, pp. 84–85

The few bits of really good comment [in *The Spirit of Romance*] are too rare to be worth hunting for. The book ... does not bear a trace of synthetic criticism of any sort; and the spirit of romance appears only in the title.

Review, unsigned, in *The Nation*, 2 March 1910

[*The Spirit of Romance*] is restlessly opinionated. He has, or desires to have, an opinion upon everything; and if he has not then his eccentric speech makes it appear that he has. He relies, in fact, as much upon his personality as upon his learning.... [And] his personality is negative, and rises to the appearance of being positive only by contradiction.... He cannot combine the scholar and the man.

Edward Thomas, in The Morning Post, 1 August 1910

A noble ambition is revealed by Mr Pound in this volume [*The Spirit of Romance*]...Mr Pound is a man of clear insight and happy enthusiasm, who is potentially a great critic. But within him there is a hunger for publicity which weakens the fibre of his work.... To find himself he must first get lost.

E. J. O., in The Boston Evening Transcript, 1910,
as cited by Stock, The Life of Ezra Pound, p. 89

We began the examination of this book of poems [*Provenca*] with great expectations and we lay it down with considerable contempt for the bulk of English criticism that has pretended to discover in these erratic utterances the voice of a poet.

William S. Braithwaite,
in The Boston Evening Transcript, 7 December 1910

It was an intense literary atmosphere, which though it was thrilling, every minute of it, was fatiguing in the extreme. I don't know how Ezra Pound stood it, it would have killed me in a month.

William Carlos Williams, Autobiography, p. 117

1911

The only thing which can justify Ezra Pound is Ezra Pound.... Ezra Pound is a true poet; his singing has distinctive spiritual and stylistic qualities which command the most respectful attention; and to those who approach his work in some humility of spirit is capable of giving a deep aesthetic satisfaction.

Floyd Dell, in *The Chicago Evening Post*, 6 January 1911

Critics praised his two earlier volumes: and as a result we now have a third [*Canzoni*] possessing the same qualities as the others. Of these qualities the bad almost totally eclipse the good. The volume ought never to have been printed...Mr. Pound has the poet in him; but he will never do anything worth preserving till he abandons his eccentricities. A genius should not covet the brain-twists, and their productions, of the lunatic!

Charles Granville, in *The Eye-Witness*, 10 August 1911

The Americans, young literary men, whom I know found him surly, supercilious and grumpy. I liked him myself very much, that is, I liked his look and air, and the few things he said, for tho' I was a good while in his company he said very little.

J. B. Yeats to W. B. Yeats, 11 February 1911

I found Ezra waiting for me on the pavement outside the house, off Oxford Circus [London], where I had a room. His appearance was...unexpected, unpredictable. He began, "I as your nearest male relation...," and hailed a taxi. He pushed me in. He banged with his stick, pounding (*Pounding*), ..."You are not going with them [a friend and her husband, who were going to the Continent]."...Awkwardly, at Victoria Station, I explained...that I wasn't coming. I had changed my mind. Awkwardly, the husband handed me back the cheque that I had made out for my ticket. Glowering and savage, Ezra waited till the train pulled out.

H. D., *End of Torment*, pp. 8–9.

Alida Monro [Mrs. Harold M.] remembered travelling one day by underground to Golders Green in the same [subway] carriage as a remarkable young man in a velvet suit. "You couldn't help noticing him."...When told of this memory, Pound replied, "Coat, not suit. Grey velvet."

Patricia Hutchins, *Ezra Pound's Kensington*, p. 130.

The pale thing we commonly call beauty is seldom in [his poems]. They are rough, uncouth, hairy, barbarous, wild. But once the galloping swing of them is mastered, a sort of stark heathenish music emerges from the noise ... [and] it is once more the springtime of the world

H. L. Mencken, in *The Smart Set*, April 1911

Another evening they had a party for us at which Millard Ashton, one of our friends, much to dear Ezra's annoyance, was acting the clown. At dessert and the passing around of ice cream and cake, said Ezra to the young man, "A special portion with arsenic is being prepared for you in the kitchen."

William Carlos Williams, *Autobiography*, p. 129

Mr. Pound decks up and cumbers his Pegasus to such an extent with this jingling and antique saddlery that it is only very rarely we can see the steed for its harness. ... Mr. Pound's work is too egotistic and not individual enough. By much the greater part of his volume is at least one remove from reality—from his own reality.

Review of *Canzoni*, unsigned,
in *The Westminister Gazette*, 19 August 1911

Each of his books so far has given us a part of his genius; some day we hope he will give us all at once.

G. D. H. Cole, in *Isis*, 4 November 1911

He is a genuine artist with eyes of his own and brains of his own, who will manage to express something strong and living whatever materials he uses, but who would gain and not lose if he could forget all about the poets of Dante's day ... and walk out of the library into the fresh air.

J. C. Squire, *The New Age*, 21 December 1911

1912

The authentic note of poetry sounds throughout this last book of Mr. Ezra Pound's [*Canzoni*]. But is he the instrument, or is he the wind in the instrument? So much of his inspiration seems bookish . . . [Yet it is] the true note of poetry.

F. S. Flint, in *Poetry Review*, January 1912

It is difficult to justify the appearance of this new translation of Guido Cavalcanti's lyrics. . . . Accuracy and care has never been harmful to true art, and Mr. Pound himself knows it quite well. . . . [But] either Mr. Pound knows very little about the Italian language, or he is totally lacking in that critical judgment necessary to the translator.

Arundel del Re, in *Poetry Review*, July 1912

Mr Ezra Pound, the young Philadelphia poet whose recent distinguished success in London led to wide recognition in his own country, authorizes the statement that at present such of his poetic work as receives magazine publication in America will appear exclusively in *Poetry*.

Harriet Monroe, in *Poetry*, October 1912

Ezra Pound was a very young man I remember when I knew him first in 1912, and how very striking he was, his personality, his dress even; he dressed congruously with himself, very unusually you see, very remarkably and full of colour. You couldn't help noticing his dress as it matched him exactly. He was a very good looking young man.

Louis Marlow Wilkinson,
BBC Third Programme,
1 February 1964

Pound's whole notion of his role as poet, critic, and impressario . . . is implicit in this long letter [to Harriet Monroe]. He is the one honest man in a world that has lost all definition and all vitality, blurred by indifference, hypocrisy, and compromise. . . . [And] Pound rather enjoys the role of revolutionary outcast.

Ellen Williams, *Harriet Monroe
and the Poetry Renaissance*, pp. 35–36

The great risk of Pound's poetry is the symbolic for its own sake. He has educated himself on old books and never correlated them. A good poet though.

T. E. Lawrence to his mother, 12 September 1912

1913

Ezra Pound, we salute you!

You are the most enchanting poet alive.... There is no mistake about you ... You are a creator of beauty in a world where only by a divinely creative process does beauty exist. (Quarrelsome poet, do not stop to discuss the matter now; besides your prose is not convincing, anyway.)

Floyd Dell, in The Chicago Evening Post
Literary Review, 4 April 1913

My dazzling friend Ezra Pound ... [His] review [of Frost's *A Boy's Will*] is a little too personal. I don't mind his calling me raw. He is reckoned raw himself and at the same time perhaps the most prominent of the younger poets here [in England].

Robert Frost to John T. Bartlett,
4 April and 16 June 1913

You will be amused to hear that Pound has taken to bullying me on the strength of what he did for me by his review in Poetry. The fact that he discovered me gives him the right to see that I live up to his good opinion of me. He says that I must write something much more like *vers libre* or he will let me perish of neglect. He really threatens.... Still I think he has meant to be generous.

Robert Frost to Thomas B. Mosher, 17 July 1913

Pound's enthusiasm for Frost was perfectly genuine.... When he found people who struck him as vividly "Amur'kn," he was overcome by an itch to instruct and correct.

Ellen Williams, Harriet Monroe
and the Poetry Renaissance, p. 67

The criticism I got . . . has given me new life and I . . . am writing with new confidence. Ezra . . . is full of the middle ages and helps me to get back to the definite and the concrete away from modern abstractions. To talk over a poem with him is like getting you to put a sentence into dialect. All becomes clear and natural. Yet in his own work he is very uncertain, often very bad though very interesting sometimes. He spoils himself by too many experiments and has more sound principles than taste.

W. B. Yeats to Lady Gregory,
3 January 1913

Although I do not really like with my whole soul the metrical experiments he has made for you, I think those experiments show a vigorous imaginative mind. He is certainly a creative personality of some sort, though it is too soon yet to say of what sort. His experiments are perhaps errors, I am not certain; but I would always sooner give the laurel to vigorous errors than to any orthodoxy not inspired.

W. B. Yeats to Harriet Monroe,
quoted from Stock,
The Life of Ezra Pound, p. 145

I think it would really be much better for you to go on with Ezra and put up with his artistic irritations; because he was really sending you jolly good stuff. That is the main thing to be considered, isn't it?

Ford Madox Hueffer [Ford]
to Harriet Monroe,
12 November 1913

John Alford in 1913 [praised] Pound—these were the days before his crankiness overshadowed other aspects of his personality—as "a unique phenomenon for he has succeeded in being an American, a man of culture, and a poet, all at the same time."

Stanley Weintraub,
The London Yankees, p. 9

I wish you would send to Ezra Pound [address omitted] three or four copies of my poems, and send me the bill for them. I owe him something like a sovereign, which the *Smart Set* sent him as commission, for getting them my two stories. This commission he sent on to me "as being averse from returning anything to the maw of an editor, and unable to take commission on my work!"—I didn't want Pound's pound of commission. So now he says he would like three or four copies of the poems, to get them into the hands of the members of the Polignac prize committee, or some such reason. The Hueffer-Pound faction seems inclined to lead me round a little as one of their show-dogs. . . . I don't care.

D. H. Lawrence to Edward Garnett,
30 December 1913

[Imagism is] a new school of English poetry still at present very small and under the formidable dictatorship of Ezra Pound.

Harold Monro [?],
in *Poetry and Drama*, June 1913

The Editor [Harriet Monroe], or at least the Editor and Mr. Pound, are using *Poetry* too egotistically . . . Propagandism has no place in a magazine of this sort. . . . Why must we accept Mr. Pound's views as final? Because his voice is loud and insistent, louder than ours? . . . He writes good poetry, when he is not too intent upon writing good poetry, for which I am one among many who are grateful. But . . . must we share all of Mr. Pound's growing pains with him, pang by pang?

Conrad Aiken to the Editor of *Poetry*, January 1913

I have just met the erratic young poet, Ezra Pound. He is the oddest youth, clever, fearfully conceited, &, at the same time, excessively thin-skinned; & I imagine that never, since the days of Wilde, have such garments been seen in the streets of London. He arrays himself like the traditional "poet" of the theater.

Amy Lowell to Carl Engel,
quoted from Jean Gould, *Any*, p. 117

In his own particular domain of poetry, however—to judge from the discontented progressive nature of the poet—no one need be astonished if, after having passed through the various stages of his wide-ranged development and manifold experiment, he shall achieve something altogether new and distinctly his own, just as in the art of painting a certain distinguished countryman of Pound's succeeded in being Whistler...

> John Cournos, in *The Philadelphia Record*,
> 5 January 1913

The bays that formerly old Dante crowned
Are worn today by Ezra Loomis Pound.

> *Punch*, 22 January 1913

Young American poetry...is divided into four schools...[one of which is] the Romantic, a body of youths who worship Ezra Pound!

> Rupert Brooke to
> Edward Marsh, 6–10 June 1913

1914

Dear Mr Pound,

Many thanks for your letter of the other day. I am afraid that I must say frankly that I do not think I can open the Columns of the *Quarterly Review*—at any rate, at present—to anyone associated publicly with such a publication as *Blast*. It stamps a man too disadvantageously.... Of course, having accepted your paper on the *Noh*, I could not refrain from publishing it. But other things would be in a different category.

> G. W. Prothero to Ezra Pound,
> 22 October 1914,
> quoted from Noel Stock,
> *The Life of Ezra Pound*, p. 162

Eliot was stimulated and encouraged by Pound's enthusiasm. Pound energized Eliot at a time when he was more or less resigned to an academic career in philosophy and turned him firmly back to a career as a poet.... "He would cajole, and almost coerce, other men into writing well," Eliot remembered, "so that he often presents the appearance of a man trying to convey to a very deaf person the fact that the house is on fire." Eliot allowed Pound to groom him as a sophisticated poet ...

Lyndall Gordon, *Eliot's Early Years*, p. 67

Mr Pound is one of the gentlest, most modest, bashful, kind creatures who ever walked the earth; so I cannot help thinking that all this enormous arrogance and petulance and fierceness are a pose. And it is a wearisome pose.

Richard Aldington,
in *The Egoist*, 15 July 1914

He [Conrad Aiken] showed me ... *Exultations* and *Personae*. He said, "This is up your street; you ought to like this." Well, I didn't really. It seemed to me rather fancy old-fashioned romantic stuff.... I wasn't very impressed by it.

T. S. Eliot, quoted from Stanley Weintraub,
The London Yankees, p. 347

Pound had elected himself teacher extraordinary to the youngest generation of poets, and not a few of Amy Lowell's later difficulties with him came from her refusal to recognize his selfless devotion to that task.

Horace Gregory, *Amy Lowell*, p. 103

When I returned to London from Ireland, I had a young man go over all my work with me to eliminate the abstract. This was the American poet Ezra Pound.

W. B. Yeats, in *Poetry*, 1914

1915

The poems in *Cathay* are things of a supreme beauty. What poetry should be, that they are.

Ford Madox Hueffer [Ford],
in *The Outlook*, 19 June 1915

Ezra's new book "Cathay" is full of the most beautiful things. I have seldom read anything finer. What a pity the boy does not confine himself to working and leave strictures on other people's work alone.

Amy Lowell to Harriet Monroe, April 1913

I fear I am going to suffer a good deal at home by the support of Pound. This is a generous person who is doing his best to put me in the wrong light by his reviews of me. . . . He made up his mind in the short time I was friends with him (we quarreled in six weeks) to add me to his party of literary refugees in London. . . . It was not in anger that I came to England and there was no shaking of dust off my feet. Pound is trying to drag me into his ridiculous row with everybody over there. I feel sorry for him for by this time he has nearly every man's hand against him on both continents and I wouldn't want to hurt him. . . . Pound sought me in every instance. He *asked* for the poem he speaks of and then failed to sell it. It was even worse than that. I had demanded the poem back when I learned the name of the magazine he was offering it to but he went ahead in spite of me. And there began our quarrel.

Robert Frost to Sidney Cox, 2 January 1915

No I haven't seen Pound's letter. What new terms of abuse has he found for your review? Why would you review him? He needs letting alone. The English have ceased to give him space in their papers.

Robert Frost to Stanley Braithwaite, 24 August 1915

The literary alliances and friendships upon which [Pound] had built his influence had been weakened ... by his own fractiousness.... He was becoming more isolated, and his own creative work was suffering as well....As early as October 1914, publishers' doors were beginning to close ...

Stanley Weintraub, The London Yankees, pp. 365–366

1916

If I were driven to name one individual who, in the English language, by means of his own examples of creative art in poetry has done most of living men to incite new impulses in poetry, the chances are I would name Ezra Pound.

Carl Sandburg, in Poetry, February 1916

Ezra Pound—yes—I am for him stronger than ever since this last sheaf in Poetry: he is so doggone deliberate and mocking and masterly in many of his pieces: ...if only his letters and personal relationships had the big ease and joy of life his art has I would hit it off great with him.

Carl Sandburg to Alice Corbin Henderson,
16 September 1916

Most of Mr Pound's original poems are in the same loose form, but he has not learned from his Chinese originals, and from his success in translating them, what kind of matter his form requires to justify it. The Chinese poems are full of content ... interesting to everyone.... But in Mr Pound's original poems ... he expresses any chance whim of his own, any liking, or more often dislike, that he happens to have experienced.... His verse is not ordinary speech, but he aims at the illusion of ordinary speech; and, although this illusion gives an air of liveliness to his poems, it seems to us to be bought at too high a price.

Review of Lustra, unsigned, in
The Times Literary Supplement, 16 November 1916

Mr Pound wrote to me in Trieste in 1913, offering his help. He brought the MSS of my novel to *The Egoist* where it was published serially . . . He also arranged for the publication in America and England. He has written many articles (all most friendly and appreciative) about me in English and American papers. But for his friendly help . . . my novel would still be unpublished.

James Joyce to
Harriet Shaw Weaver,
8 November 1916

Why, why will you needlessly irritate people?

Elkin Mathews to Ezra Pound,
quoted from Eric Homberger, *Ezra Pound*

The area was "prohibited," and Pound discovered after a time that he should have registered as an alien. Yeats reported that after his third visit from a policeman Pound had flung out of the house so violently that he had torn the coat hook from the wall.

B. L. Reid, *The Man
From New York*, p. 241

1917

[The] almost excessive air of detachment about Ezra Pound's work gives an impression of coldness, of almost bitter aloofness from the common run. His rebelliousness is purely aesthetic and intellectual, however, against stupidity, banality—one suspects—against simplicity itself. He is determined to accept no emotion at its face value—and accepts none. Without emotion, he does not move one.

G. W. Cronin, in
New York Call Magazine,
23 December 1917

Pound is not one of those poets who make no demands of the reader; and the casual reader of verse, disconcerted by the difference between Pound's poetry and that on which his taste has been trained, attributes his own difficulties to excessive scholarship on the part of the author.

T. S. Eliot, Ezra Pound: His Metric and His Poetry (1917),
as reprinted in Eliot, To Criticize the Critic, p. 166

I've had correspondence with Ezra and have reveled in his ingenuity of insult, which same I met with ribald joshing. He desisted because he couldn't make me as mad as he got himself. He is a most thorny and knobby person but there is some substance to him.

William M. Reedy to Babette Deutsch,
22 November 1917

He is a modern of the moderns...the Zeno of the twentieth century...But he is yet a rebel thinker...

Babette Deutsch, in Reedy's Mirror, 21 December 1917

Pound apparently had no sharp intuition of Harriet Monroe's identity. Throughout their long relationship, he seems unclear about her attitudes and reactions. As late as 1917, he questioned Alice Corbin Henderson whether Miss Monroe took him seriously.

Ellen Williams, Harriet Monroe
and the Poetry Renaissance, p. 74

I haven't sufficient belief in the infallibility of Ezra Pound's mind to require no substantiation of his statements....He's a bit too easily swayed by his personal emotions...[and] he has, also, too great a longing to separate poets into arbitrary terms of best and worse. Poets are either black or white to him— never grey.

Maxwell Bodenheim, in The Little Review, June 1917

There has been an odd insistence in the way Pound has evoked the domination of the great writers. With the exception of those old writers who influenced him in his youth, he has treated other poets with a savage familiarity. I can believe that some of his inspirers might have found him disturbing, rather intemperate, often impertinent.

Jean de Bosschere, in *The Egoist*, 1917

As he was leaving for his honeymoon Yeats asked Pound to send a telegram about the wedding to Lady Gregory at Coole Park. But suddenly reflecting upon the nature of the event and the breadth of Pound's creative faculties and epistolary style, he thoughtfully added: "*Not* one that will be talked about in Coole for the next generation."

Quoted from Noel Stock, *The Life of Ezra Pound*, p. 211

That boy of mine is always springing some surpise.

Homer Pound to John Quinn, 26 October 1917

He is a powerful astringent. he may inflict pain, but his pain is salutary. It is wonderful how people who do not know him hate him. I sometimes think that opposition, even hatred, is the harvest he wants to gather.

John Quinn to Vincent O'Sullivan, 22 November 1917

"Oh," said Willie [William Butler Yeats] sadly, "he is violent by conviction."

Lily Yeats to John Quinn, 1 June 1917

1918

He has always a ton of precept for a pound of example....But in the long run and for the cultivation of poetry as an art there is no doubt that the most fruitful way is the way of the craftsman and the adept.

A. R. Orage, in *The New Age*, 25 July 1918

At this moment in an unusual career, the American-born Pound seemed bent on fostering other talents than easing his own struggles in the world. This zeal caused Gertrude Stein to call him "a village explainer, excellent if you were a village, but if you were not, not."

Allen Churchill,
The Improper Bohemians, p. 128

This [*Pavannes and Divisions*] is the record of a creative talent grown sterile, of a disorderly retreat into the mazes of technique and pedantry . . . [a] collection of out of date manifestoes and poorly disguised platitudes. . . . And so the reckless poet of 1910 develops into the sophisticated poseur; . . . he becomes the scholiast gone to seed.

Louis Untermeyer, in
The New Republic, 17 August 1918

I fear you are right about Pound. . . . Puritan pressure has converted him into a mere bellower. There is a lesson in this for all of us.

H. L. Mencken to Louis Untermeyer,
21 August 1918, *Letters of H. L. Mencken*, p. 127

The outstanding feature of this book of prose [*Pavannes and Divisions*] is its dullness. . . . It is difficult to imagine anything much worse than the prose of Mr. Pound. It is ugliness and awkwardness incarnate. . . . Mr. Pound has become, as regards style, a purist of the most deadly sort.

Conrad Aiken, in *The Dial*, October 1918

We could annotate nearly every page of the book [*Pavannes and Divisions*] with eager agreement or dissent. This means that it is worth reading. You may wish that you had Mr Pound before you in the flesh, to tell him what you think of him; but that, no doubt, is exactly the effect he wishes to produce on you.

Review, unsigned, in *The Times Literary Supplement*, 19 September 1918

Not that I've read more than 10 words by Ezra Pound but my conviction of his humbug is unalterable....I was so rash as to say to [T. S.] Eliot the other night that Wyndham Lewis and Ezra Pound were the biggest humbugs unhung, and then had to own that this was mere inspiration on my part, as I have never read a word of either of them.

Virginia Woolf to Roger Fry, 18 November 1918,
and to Duncan Grant, 29 November 1918

Whether we agree or not with his opinions, we may be always sure that in his brief and fugitive utterances he is not to be diverted on any pretext from the essential literary problem, that he is always concerned with the work of art, never with incidental fancies.

T. S. Eliot, review of *Pavannes and Divisions*,
in *The Egoist*, November-December 1918

My complaint against Ezra is that, having attracted me time and again with the promise of delightful cerebral embraces, he is forever bidding me adieu with no more than a languid handshake—a suave, fastidious, an irreproachable, but still a handshake....He does not present to me a style—but a series of portrayals....To me Pound remains the exquisite showman minus a show.

Ben Hecht, in *The Little Review*, November 1918

I like a fight but I admit that I have at times objected to your promptness with the cudgels.

Marianne Moore to Ezra Pound, December 1918

E. P. is certainly a poet but I am afraid I am too old and too wooden-headed to appreciate him as perhaps he deserves. The critics here consider him harmless; but as he has, I believe, a very good opinion of himself I don't suppose he worries his head about the critics very much. Besides, he has many women at his feet; which must be immensely comforting.

Joseph Conrad to John Quinn, 6 February 1918

1919

More and more am I turning toward Pound and Eliot and the minor Elizabethans for values.

Hart Crane to Gorham Munson, 27 December 1919

Pound's critical exposition was often fuzzy, though his intuitive taste was keen; my friends and I admired his early volumes of lyrics, *Personae* and *Lustra*, for their terse, stripped-down, neo-classical language, which made Ezra Pound unique among poets writing in English—our great "decadent" as we called him then.... [He] ruled over the circle of Imagist poets in London like a king in exile.

Matthew Josephson, Life Among
the Surrealists, pp. 61, 63

If Mr. Pound were a professor of Latin, there would be nothing left for him but suicide.... I beg him to lay aside the mask of erudition.

W. G. Hale, in Poetry, April 1919

He hurtles himself into the decorous St. Faith's Nursing Home, in Ealing, near London. Beard, black soft had, ebony stick—something unbelievably operatic—directoire overcoat, Verdi. He stalked and stamped the length of the room. He coughed, choked or laughed... He seemed to beat with the bony stick like a baton. I can't remember. Then there is a sense of his pounding, pounding (*Pounding*) with the stick against the wall. He had banged that way, with a stick once before, in a taxi, at a grave crisis in my life. This [the imminent birth of her second child] was a grave crisis in my life.... "But," he said, "my only criticism is that this is not my child."

H. D., End of Torment, pp. 7–8

Pound is frank above all things. One need not read one of his sentences twice to learn its meaning.

John Quinn to Horace Brodzky, 8 January 1919

With Pound I have the same complex . . . as when one of my children won't do something good for it which it is told to do. Pound is [a] genius of some kind.

Carl Sandburg to Louis Untermeyer, 10 April 1919

[Mencken felt that] Ezra Pound had an excellent ear and without doubt gave a thrilling poetic show. But of late [1919] he had become an angry pamphleteer, dropping "the lute for the bayonet."

Carl Bode, Mencken, p. 96

1920

This overmastering desire to exhibit every triviality, to let not one bad joke blush unseen, spoils many a bright page and most of the volume [*Lustra*]. Pound chatters on, and his wandering loquacity dulls the edge of a really keen irony. . . . Pound has gone on, collecting cultures, and all they have yielded him is an accent, an attitude. . . . He has really very little to say . . . The escape into literature is complete; the poetry is mostly dumb show, but he can still simulate life.

Louis Untermeyer, in The Dial, December 1920

Here is Mr. Pound again proferring a neglectful world a new volume, this time divided into four sections and varying in merit from his best to his abominable worst: all with the Poundian flavour more pronounced than ever. . . . More and more as we read we become aware of the Poundian personality: that queer compost of harsh levity, spite, cocksureness, innuendo, pedantry, archaism, sensuality, real if sometimes perverse and unfortunate research and honest love of literature.

Robert Nichols, in The Observer, 11 January 1920

Yes, Pound is right in what he says in his "The Rest,"—"O helpless few in my country, O remnant enslaved! . . . You who cannot wear yourselves out by persisting to successes."

Hart Crane to Gorham Munson, 20 October 1920

The first of the exiles in point of time, and perhaps also in eminence, is Ezra Pound. . . . [But Pound] can only get life out of books—from the life about him, he can obtain nothing.

John Gould Fletcher,
in *Chapbook*, May 1920

The intellectual perversity of Ezra Pound has disgusted many of his contemporaries. His influence on the younger poetry of our day is least admitted by many who have been most subject to it. The recognition of his genius will be gradual and tardy . . .

Harold Monro,
Some Contemporary Poets, p. 87

There never was a poet more susceptible to influence, more sensitive to cadences, to the subtle flavors and flying gestures of words . . . He has adopted the mask of fantastic intellectual Inhumanism. . . . All the approaches to this twentieth century poet are difficult, . . . but in this immense and hospitable universe there is room . . . for the clear hardness, the civilised polished beauty, the Augustan irony of Ezra Pound.

May Sinclair, in
The North American Review, May 1920

It is quite astonishing still to find young and intelligent persons who can not forgive Ezra Pound for living in England and sticking out his tongue at his native land . . . [for] Ezra Pound has very much at heart the civilization of these United States. And I am sure he has done more for the new literature in this country than many of those who claim a proprietary right over it. . . . [Yet] Ezra Pound has inhabited for a long time a universe that consists mainly of . . . themes of [a very] limited sort which, if they are pursued too long, turn the best of talkers into a bore. In the name of literature, what can be done to prevent Ezra Pound from becoming a bore?

Van Wyck Brooks,
in *the Freeman*, 16 June 1920

Dear Ezra: Your heart is golden: so are yr. words. But the latter are normally—even when they can be read—incomprehensible.

Ford Madox Hueffer [Ford] to E. P., 27 July 1920

Be it said of this peppy gentleman that, insofar as he is responsible for possibly one-half of the most alive poetry and probably all of the least intense prose committed, during the last few years, in the American and English language, he merits something beyond the incoherent abuse and inchoate adoration which have become his daily breakfast food.

E. E. Cummings, *A Miscellany Revised*, p. 27

He is perhaps the most extraordinary man that American literature has seen in our time, and, characteristically enough, he keeps as far away from America as possible.

H. L. Mencken, in *The Smart Set*, August 1920

The real difference between Mr. Pound and most of the poets of his time is that he is individual and imaginative with distinction....It is a sort of fastidious vigour: a subtle form of strength.

Edwin Muir, in *The New Age*, 22 July 1920

You and I can swear in writing at each other, and talk and write straight from the shoulder, whereas some of these younger fellows don't understand it.

John Quinn to Ezra Pound, 1 May 1920

For a man such as Quinn all years were hard, but 1920 was perhaps especially so. One of the reasons for Quinn's warm personal feeling for Ezra Pound was that Pound was one of the few friends and beneficiaries among the artists [that Quinn patronized so freely] who seemed to feel, and occasionally to show, some insight and sympathy for the continual tension of Quinn's professional life.

B. L. Reid, *The Man From New York*, p. 457

1921

About the only thing to be gathered from Pound's article on Brancusi is that Pound wishes to avoid being obvious at the cost of no matter what else.

Hart Crane to Gorham Munson, 21 November 1921

Mr. Ezra Pound is a man of my own height, reddish goatee and ear whiskers, heavier built, moves nicely, temperament very similar to J. Sibley Watson Jr. . . . —same timidity and subtlety, not nearly so inhibited. Altogether, for me, a gymnastic personality. Or in other words somebody, and intricate. . . . During our whole promenade Ezra was more than wonderfully entertaining: he was magically gentle, as only a great man can be toward some shyest child.

E. E. Cummings to his parents, 23 July 1921, and to Charles Norman, 21 January 1959

When Amy Lowell and Ezra Pound fail to make good poems, in spite of their comprehensive knowledge of the art of poetry, it is quite probably because they are creating according to theory and not as [a] result of genuine feeling. It is difficult to write about [Pound]. He is so clever that one mentions him with trepidation, knowing how amused he would be at the wrong thing said. The truth of the matter is that Mr. Pound is too clever to be a poet. He ought to spend his time in discovering geniuses and explaining talent and genius to a less clever world. For whether one agrees with him or not, he is frequently interesting as a critic. . . . Very likely Mr. Pound does not expect or even wish his poems to give pleasure to many readers. He would prefer, probably, to please a few hundred carefully selected intellects. Or perhaps he would please only himself and is content to amuse the dull world.

Marguerite Wilkinson, *New Voices*, pp. 54, 183

1922

Ezra Pound, with much tumult and shouting, buried the dry bones of the past and sounded their tocsin for a new era.

Harriet Monroe, in *Poetry*, October 1922

The real value of the *Waste Land* manuscript, [Eliot] judged, lay in its evidences of the work of Ezra Pound's expert obstetric hand—"worth preserving in its present form solely for the reason that it is the only evidence of the difference which his criticism has made to this poem."

T. S. Eliot to John Quinn, 21 September 1922, quoted
from B. L. Reid, *The Man From New York* , pp. 539–540

Pound even then seemed to be living in a world of his own illusions, formed by the books he was reading in Provencal, Italian, or Chinese; the *Cantos* themselves were in part a pastiche of his bookish borrowings, and divorced from the realities of this world.

Matthew Josephson, *Life Among the Surrealists*, p. 89

The massive isolation of Ezra Pound has probably not been surpassed by that of any other poet in any other generation, and seldom equalled. . . . His opaque isolation is one of carved metal standing apart from the thin transparencies of a contemporary world.

Maxwell Bodenheim, in *The Dial*, January 1922

Ezra Pound's new book of poems—*Poems 1918-21*—is as unsatisfactory as his previous ones. . . . He has not even yet, in his original work, really mastered his own style, which still remains patchy and uneven and acutely self-conscious. . . . Ezra Pound's aesthetic ideal is probably one of the highest in contemporary poetry in English. Indifferent to public approval, he has labored conscientiously and fiercely to reduce the vague substance of words to a sharp hard residuum of beauty . . . but the trouble is that all his lines are isolated lines. His poems do not hang together. . . . There is a strange discrepancy between Pound's ideals and his ability to embody them in his work.

Edmund Wilson, *The Shores of Light*, pp. 44–45

I sincerely consider Ezra Pound the most important living poet in the English language.

T. S. Eliot to Gilbert Seldes, quoted
from Stock, *The Life of Ezra Pound*, p. 249

I've been teaching Pound to box wit little success. He habitually leads wit his chin and has the general grace of the crayfish ... It's pretty sporting of him to risk his dignity and his critical reputation at something that he don't know nothing about. He's really a good guy, Pound, wit a fine bitter tongue onto him.

Ernest Hemingway to Sherwood Anderson,
9 March 1922

Mr. Pound knows perhaps better than any living American what poetry should be.

John Peale Bishop, in Vanity Fair, January 1922

Tell me more of Pound. We recently had from him an ill-spelled, ill-written, ill-phrased, idiotic letter enclosing an incoherent and all but illegible article. He spoke of having seen you. If you see him again, don't encourage him to do any more articles for us.

Edmund Wilson to John Peale Bishop,
5 September 1922

I am in correspondence with Ezra Pound. A complete muddle, as you may imagine.

Virginia Woolf to Roger Fry, 22 October 1922

1923

As you may know, I have for some years been an admirer of Pound's poetry: personally, he sometimes gives me a Father Complex.

E. E. Cummings to his mother, 24 October 1923

Aldington says we must communicate with Pound. He has quarrelled with Pound and wants you or me to write. I will do this, if you like—unless you know him, and could make him say what money he has got, and what their plans are. I have never seen him; and only hate his works.

Virginia Woolf to Lady Ottoline Morrell, 24 September 1923

Pound I should like sometime to see again just for the pleasure of quarreling with him. His articles in *The Dial* infuriate me!

Conrad Aiken to Malcolm Cowley, 26 March 1923

1924

Ezra Pound [is] a talent, but has he written more than one lyric (you know, we're talking about lyrics not epigrams after Martial and Catullus, valuable and worthy as they are)?

Burton Rascoe, quoted from
Charles Norman, *E. E. Cummings*, p. 190

Brancusi served us cognac, poked up the fire and then began talking of Ezra Pound's recent "opera," *Villon* ... "Pound writing an opera?" I said. "Why, he doesn't know one note from another." Brancusi was furious ...

William Carlos Williams, *Autobiography*, p. 188

Ezra goes to Italy for good on Sunday. He has indulged in a small nervous breakdown necessitating him spending two days at the Am. Hospital during the height of the packing.

Ernest Hemingway to Gertrude Stein
and Alice B. Toklas, 10 October 1924

1925

Not long ago Mr. Pound galloped up and down the frontier of criticism like an early American general, cursing the enemy, firing his recruits, and embarrassing the fearless with decorations of praise. The gallant fighter appears to have withdrawn from the hubbub.

Glenway Westcott, in *The Dial*, December 1925

Ezra Pound ... by his creative work, his editorship of several magazines, his helpful friendship for young and unknown artists ... comes first to our mind as meriting the gratitude of this generation.

Ernest Walsh and Ethel Moorhead,
in *This Quarter*, Spring 1925

He has wide knowledge, with strange gaps of ignorance, especially when he leaves the one subject he really knows—i.e., poetry. Possibly his credulity in matters of occultism and economics, for example, is due to a complete lack of the philosophical training so conspicuous in T. S. Eliot.

Richard Aldington, in *This Quarter*,
Autumn–Winter 1925

1926

But even turning out poor writing was better than getting "all full of romance and ingrown literature" like Ezra Pound.

Townsend Ludington, *John Dos Passos*, p. 255

1927

He is the swashbuckler of the Arts. I rather wish he was not. But ... if there is an abuse to remedy Ezra discharges a broadside of invective in unusual jargon at the head of the oppressor.... Instead of drugs he stupifies himself with the narcotics of reform. In that he is very American—but what a poet!

Ford Madox Ford, in *N.Y. Herald Tribune*,
9 January 1927

Pound has too many rules. The rules of revolution are as revolting as the rules of reaction. And there are more of them.... Pound is crazy. Last letter he asked me to learn Arabic so as to write like myself.... I'm getting a bit fed up with the Ezraic assumption that he is a Great Man. Let the rest of us say so for a while.... Don't expect anything of Pound. He's cucku. A foin pote but no critic.... I don't get your angle on Pound. Is obsession with *The Past* equivalent to Bergsonian-Whiteheadian-Alexandrian-Time-Duree obsession?

Archibald MacLeish to Robert N. Linscott, 5 January 1927,
to Ernest Hemingway, 14 February 1927,
to Allen Tate, 16 February 1927, and
to Wyndham Lewis, December 1927

Pound is not a modernist..., as any one who stays at home must be, in that he does not accept, has not accepted, his local material to make it "beautiful." Instead, he fights his material, selects too finely sometimes....Pound is full of beauty for people of intelligence—only part of it comes off in verse—sometimes I think not the best part. Pound is inarticulate....[He] has sought to communicate his poetry to us and failed. It is a tragedy, since he is our best poet.

William Carlos Williams, in *The New York*
Evening Post Literary Review, 19 February 1927

This Quarter...dedicated itself to the religion of literature, and acknowledged Ezra Pound as its patron saint—but soon the editors agrily disavowed Mr. Pound. ["I herewith take back that dedication," wrote Miss Moorhead, Mr. Walsh having died. "I have said before that Ernest Walsh was disillusioned about Ezra Pound before he died. *We* take back our too-generous dedication."]

Matthew Josephson, *Life Among the Surrealists*, p. 321,
and Noel Stock, *The Life of Ezra Pound*, p. 261

What is personal in his work is the general tone infusing his various styles; and the ultimate value of his poetry should be in the adequacy of his methods and the freshness of his ways of feeling, rather than in the novelty or truth of his substance....Without great original genius, Pound has made more *poetry* than most of his contemporaries; because he has understood better than almost anyone what poetry is not...

R. P. Blackmur, in *The Saturday Review*
of Literature, April 1927

It is possible Pound is right but I cannot go back. I never listened to his objections to *Ulysses*...He understood certain aspects of that book very quickly and that was more than enough then. He makes brilliant discoveries and howling blunders.

James Joyce to Harriet Shaw Weaver,
1 February 1927

There is nothing that he intuits well, certainly never originally. Yet when he can get into the skin of somebody else, of power and renown, a Propertius or an Arnaut Daniel, he becomes a lion or a lynx on the spot.

Wyndham Lewis, in *The Enemy*, February 1927

1928

I confess I am seldom interested in what Pound . . . is saying, but only in the way he says it.

T. S. Eliot, in *The Dial*, 1928

I had the whim to publish an "Open Letter to Ezra Pound," urging him to return to the United States. "We have learned much from you, and I shall not be one of those who deny it," I began. But his idea of the poet's function was still that of the 1890 decadents. He was striking attitudes, making words play with each other.

Matthew Josephson, *Life Among the Surrealists*, p. 364

The Dial Award for 1927 was recently offered to Mr Ezra Pound, and we are most happy to announce that he accepted it—with this proviso: "It is impossible for me to accept an award except on Cantos or on my verse as a whole. . . ." We agreed to the proviso without hesitation, indeed we had never any different notion about it.

James Watson, in *The Dial*, January 1928

Ezra Pound has been helping me to punctuate my new poems . . . He has . . . [Maud Gonne's] passion for cats and large numbers wait him every night at a certain street corner knowing that his pocket is full of meat bones or chicken bones.

W. B. Yeats to Lady Gregory, February and April, 1928

1929

No one with an open mind can possibly read Mr. Pound's poetry without realizing that he is above all, a traditionalist.... [He is] the most perfect type in our time of a purely "aesthetic" poet ... [and the *Cantos*] are an anthology of all the passages in poetry of the past that Mr. Pound has been interested in ... But to say that they are a poem in any sense of the word is to say that calisthenics are essentially the same thing as the Russian ballet.... We have a right to demand something better from a serious poet than the versification of fifteenth-century (or nineteenth-century) business letters.

John Gould Fletcher,
in *The Criterion*, April 1929

I had never understood until now that the translations ... are as much a part of his original work, as much chosen as to theme, as much characterized as to style, as the vituperation, the railing, which I had hated but which now seem a necessary balance. He is not trying to create forms because he believes, like so many of his contemporaries, that old forms are dead, so much as a new style, a new man.

W. B. Yeats,
A Packet for Ezra Pound, p. 7

Thank you very much for letting us see this essay on Pound. I have read it with interest, but I think it is a little too specialized, a little too technical, for us. It is the sort of thing which really ought to appear in some poets' magazine.

Edmund Wilson to
Louis Zukofsky, 11 December 1929

1930

Ezra is so completely out of touch with America that he recently wrote one of the boys he supposed he would be lynched if he set foot in New York. Poor devil, not more than ten people would know who he was. And they would be more apt to hang him with laurel than with feathers. I admire that man so much ... [but] why can't he act like a poet? Why does he have to pamphleteer in the accents of an exasperated asp?

Archibald MacLeish to
Harriet Monroe, 29 November 1930

1931

[Pound's poetry] has had more influence on us than any other of our time; it has had an immense "underground" reputation. And deservedly.... He is probably one or two or three living Americans who will be remembered as poets of the first order.

Allen Tate, *Essays of Four Decades*, pp. 365, 370

Mr. Pound's documentation [in the *Cantos*] is a device, a technic. History and literature are for him a mine of images, and his purpose is to fix certain of these images in a lasting, orderly design, without reference to a philosophy or to any system of teleological principles.... The Cantos may be described as an epic of timelessness. It is, without any doubt, the most ambitious poetic concept of our day; and it is so nearly successful in execution that fault-finding seems invidious.... It is much more than splendid writing. It is a gallant proud attempt to assert the positive value of experience.

Dudley Fitts, in *Hound & Horn*, Winter 1931

At Pound's suggestion [Louis] Zukofsky had been invited by Harriet Monroe to edit an "Objectivists" number of *Poetry* which appeared in February 1931. It did not include work by Pound who gave over to younger poets the space offered him.

Noel Stock, *The Life of Ezra Pound*, p. 305

1932

But in essentials Mr Pound's poetry is very different from Mr Eliot's. There are in it none of Mr Eliot's complex intensities of concern about soul and body: the moral, religious and antrhopological preoccupations are absent. Mr Pound's main concern has always been art: he is, in the most serious sense of the word, an aesthete.

F. R. Leavis, *New Bearings in English Poetry*, p. 117

Although Mr. Ezra Pound's method is a cunning imitation of the pre-historical view that seized past and present naively as a whole, the *Cantos* is a monument to the historical mentality.

Allen Tate, *Essays of Four Decades*, p. 244

The Cantos have no core or central theme ... The beauty of the Cantos is like that of a frieze, is decorative rather than vital.

Henry Bamford Parkes,
in *The New English Weekly*, December 1932

Any poet born in this century or in the last ten years of the preceding century who can honestly say that he has not been influenced by or learned greatly from the work of Ezra Pound deserves to be pitied rather than rebuked.... The best of Pound's writing—and it is in the Cantos—will last as long as there is any literature.

Ernest Hemingway, in *The Cantos of Ezra Pound:
Some Testimonies...*, quoted in Carlos Baker,
Ernest Hemingway: A Life Story, p. 236

Pound is a unicorn who turns into an ass every time you look at him too closely.... Pound, in revolt, saw the evils of the romantic method ... but was blind to the fundamental Romantic vice because he was himself at heart a strutting Romantic with an ego exaggerated to the Falstaffian proportions we now observe.

Archibald MacLeish to
Louis Untermeyer, 22 June 1932,
and to Allen Tate, 9 July 1932

Pound ... meant a great deal to the writers of my generation in America. In spite of his expatriation, which I deplored, and the rather meager and bookish fare with which his poetry always seemed to be to be nourished, he was one of the few American writers of his time who represented genuinely high standards and never let us down.

Edmund Wilson to Ford Madox Ford, 13 October 1932

1933

Documentation is all right if we know what it documents. But do we—in Pound's case?

> Eda Lou Walton, in *The New York Times Book Review*, 2 April 1933

All the romantic outpourings seemed tame compared to the tough irony of Pound.

> Ronald Duncan, *All Men Are Islands*, p. 87

Remembering that the thirty Cantos are only a fragment, and affirming that many of the innumerable implications can only be understood after a more thorough study of all Mr. Pound's reading than I have carried out, I doubt still whether the Cantos have, in their splash of tints and shades, the compulsive and pervading discipline, the cellular inevitability that must belong to . . . a rounded organism. . . . I believe, in brief, that the method of the Cantos . . . is a bad one well used.

> Geoffrey Grigson, in *New Verse*, October 1933

It would be difficult to hit on a poem *more* alive than Mr. Pound's "poem of some length." Looking back on the Cantos as a whole, one is most impressed by their gusto. [Still,] if the Cantos are so written that they are more interesting as pure poetry than as significance, then they are not fulfilling their purpose.

> D. G. Bridson, in *The New English Weekly*, 5 October 1933

Mr. Pound has written a short book on Economic theory—of which he is as innocent as the well-beloved apostle. He is of course, as always, a voice crying in the wilderness.

> Archibald MacLeish to John Peale Bishop, April 1933

If there is a living man to point to as symbolic of all that has happened (both good and bad) in the evolvement of letters since the turn of the century, it is Ezra Pound.... Suffice it to say that, no matter who or what one reads, especially in contemporary French, German, and Italian, the influence of his many-sided talent is bound somewhere to emerge.

Editorial, unsigned,
in The Outrider, 1 November 1933

1934

Mr. Pound has spent his life putting effort and impudence into what people refuse to take time to enjoy or evaluate.

Marianne Moore, in The Criterion, April 1934

[*Homage to Sextus Propertius*] is the most interesting and the most sustained of his translations, and in the technique and beautiful surface it is the finest development of his early work. For Mr. Pound's writing is essentially surface writing: it contains no profundity of thought, and little obscurity of meaning. The only difficulty which it presents to the "common reader" is one of reference...It is a mistake though to suppose that this knowledge is essential to an appreciation even of the Cantos. For such poetry has an existence of its own which is independent of the writer's sources...It creates its own conditions, even while it is referring to another environment.

Stephen Spender, in The Spectator, 14 December 1934

I happen to feel that there exists one way of "helping" creators; which is, not hindering them: and that there exists one way of not hindering them; which is, abolishing "censorship"—after proudly issuing which Emancipation Proclamation, the President of the United States may humbly request Ezra Pound to take charge of America's "arts"

E. E. Cummings to Edward B. Rowan, August 1934

And now everybody has made it but Ezra.

Ernest Hemingway to
Arnold Gingrich, 15 July 1934

By a somewhat ironic fate [he] has gained his great reputation chiefly by his innovations, though it is where his work is least novel that it is most successful.

John Sparrow, Sense and Poetry, p. 122

There are two things about Mr. Pound that I like: he is very learned, which I am not; and he has furious likes and dislikes, which I have but should hesitate to state so furiously.

G. K. Chesterton, in
The Listener, 23 November 1934

I wasn't ... much surprised when Archie MacLeish vulgarized Eliot and Pound enough to get himself the Pulitzer Prize.

Edmund Wilson to
Phelps Putnam, 4 December 1934

1935

His criticism, in fact, is that rare and delightful thing, pure literary criticism ... Whatever one may think of some of Mr. Pound's conclusions, ... these collected essays [*Make It New*] are for the reader a valuable exercise in intelligent criticism, useful to the poet, but probably more useful still to the reader of poetry: they provide intellectual pleasure.

Bonamy Dobrée, in The Criterion, April 1935

The new Cantos of Mr. Pound's, XXXI to XLI, are very much like the others. If there is a difference it is that the new ones have gone a little further still from any accepted tradition of what poetry is; direr, as if a little wearier, yet more resolute than the old ones. ... What has really disappeared in the condensed poetry of Mr. Pound, of course, is both a certain spirit and a certain music, until the old product and the new differ not quantitatively but qualitatively. ... The thesis which his honorable if bewildered career suggests ... [is that the times] required another poetry, and the old poetry could not be saved.

John Crowe Ransom, in The Saturday Review
of Literature, 19 January 1935

From his private regions of poetic material he obtains stuff indigenously extraordinary by which, quite naturally, one is fascinated, if not invariably charmed. And this in itself corroborates the newness. It is because Mr. Pound has actually accomplished a discovery of new subject matter (and has not, like so many innovators, merely purloined it) that his poetry excites and presages.

George Barker, in The Criterion, July 1935

It is from the "Propertius" and "Mauberley" rather than from the Cantos that whatever of value may be learned from Mr. Pound will be learned, and . . . this is as much as to say that they are the better poems.

John Speirs, in Scrutiny, March 1935

1936

When I consider his work as a whole I find more style than form; at moments more style, more deliberate mobility and the means to convey it than in any contemporary poet known to me, but it is constantly interrupted, broken, twisted into nothing by its direct opposite, nervous obsession, nightmare, stammering confusion . . . Even where there is no interruption he is often content, if certain verses and lines have style, to leave unabridged transitions, unexplained ejaculations, that make his meaning unintelligible. . . . Even where the style is sustained throughout one gets an impression, especially when he is writing in *vers libre*, that he has not got all the wine into the bowl, that he is a brilliant improvisator translating at sight from an unknown Greek masterpiece.

W. B. Yeats, Oxford Book of Modern Verse, pp. xxv–xxvi

1937

In brief, you come to the defense of quackery too late. All you say or can say has been said 10,000 times before, and by better men.... You made your great mistake when you abandoned the poetry business, and set up shop as a wizard in general practise. You wrote, in your day, some very good verse, and I had the pleasure, along with other literary buzzards, of calling attention to it at the time. But when you fell into the hands of those London logrollers, and began to wander through pink fogs with them, all your native common sense oozed out of you, and you set up a caterwauling for all sorts of brummagem Utopias, at first in the aesthetic region only but later in the regions of political and aesthetic baloney.

> H. L. Mencken to
> Ezra Pound, 28 November 1937,
> *Letters of H. L. Mencken*, p. 411

1938

The Cantos ... are the production of one who has devoted himself almost wholly to literature, whether knowingly or not, as his ruling value.... Pound has been the pure literary man, the complete man of letters.... And when we examine the texture of the verse [in The *Cantos*], we find lacking, amid much beauty of language, other elements which have been characteristic of great poetry.... We get what is upon the surface, ... but we do not get anything more than this.

> Delmore Schwartz, in *Poetry*, March 1938

Poor Ezra ... Such travesties of what we have desired take the spirit out of my old age more than all that can be called defeat. They give me that what's-the-use feeling.... I wonder if Ezra will appreciate your effort to be temperate with what he has become in memory of what he once promised to become.

> Robert Frost to
> Louis Untermeyer, 5 February 1938

While Babbo [Ezra Pound] read out loud no one stirred. A sort of tinkle hung suspended in the air, threatening to explode if anything moved.

Mary de Rachewiltz, *Discretions*, p. 101

He became involved in a world of self-delusion over which he ruled as per regulations of his own making.

C. David Heymann, *Ezra Pound: The Last Rower*, p. 79

Only Yeats and Eliot can compare with Pound among living poets for richness of diction. And his diction is at its richest in the "Propertius."

James Laughlin, in *Sewanee Review*,
October-December 1938

1939

He was, and he still is, one of the great clearers and cleansers of cluttered earth. If a new generation does not see him in these terms it is because a new generation does not know the architecture he has overthrown. These poems which are wall ornaments now that the old buildings have gone down were tools once—hooked iron crowbars and mallet-headed sledges and cold steel chisels of destruction.

Archibald MacLeish, in *The Atlantic Monthly*, June 1939

He is all for breaking up, throwing out, biting the thumb at, pulling the beards of, disinterring, freshening, "making new." He refuses to attack moldy but sacred academic rigamaroles from a distance.... Pound walks into the field armed with stink bombs.

Louise Bogan, *A Poet's Alphabet*, p. 333

I suppose he has a better ear, a subtler, more assured feeling for language, than anyone writing today. Of his scholarship, on the other hand, one can be less sure.

Dudley Fitts, in *The Saturday Review*, 13 May 1939

Did Sibley ever see Ezra Pound? He zoomed into Patchin, all gloat and gasping against ... the heat and juggling all his mythical realities like "Possum" and "Brancoosh" and "Uncle Jarg"; but I'm very fond of Ezra ...

E. E. Cummings to Hildegarde Watson,
18 September 1939

Cummings was in bed with grippe when Pound knocked at 4 Patchin Place, but he sat up to welcome the visitor. He told me later that he—and his wife—had been extremely disconcerted by Pound's tirades, and were relieved when he left for Washington ...

Charles Norman, *E. E. Cummings*, p. 297

Carlos Williams saw Ezra by accident in Washington the other day. He says the author of the Cantos seems very mild and depressed and fearful. That is all I know about him. He has made no sign to me.

Ford Madox Ford to Allen Tate, 3 May 1939

I fear that ... in a guide to culture [*Guide to Kulchur*], this is just pure bosh in an excited tone of voice. What is he running away from?

Philip Mairet, in *The Criterion*, January 1939

What Pound is attempting brilliantly in his [*Guide to Kulchur*], for all its follies, is to cut short the awful waste of life we suffer to gain knowledge. He is attempting to make it good form to find a way to the gist of learning before we are crippled by age and cannot make use of it. The swiftness with which we get knowledge should be one of its major virtues. ... The failure of the book is that by its tests Mussolini is a great man; and the failure of Pound, that he thinks him so. The book should be read for its style, its wide view of learning ... The rest can be forgiven as the misfortune of a brave man who took the risk of making a bloody fool of himself and—lost.

William Carlos Williams,
in *The New Republic*, June 1939

1940

We have then in the Cantos an attempt to x-ray the modern mind, to go deep into it by an examination of the roots in history of its patterns of action.

James Laughlin, *Notes on Ezra Pound's Cantos*

Mr. Pound is capable of imposing style on the most heterogeneous material. As a technician there is no one to touch him.... Why Mr. Pound's criticism of human society required the inclusion of such a mass of detailed matter may become clear when the poem is finished.

Edwin Muir, in *Purpose*, July-December 1940

Mr. Pound is obviously one of the most talented poets of our time; yet these Cantos are almost unreadable.... Mr. Pound has always had likings or prejudices rather than standards—his strength has lain mainly in disconnected insights. Organization and logic have been his weak point... His talents are primarily lyric—not narrative, certainly not expository or didactic. He is not really a "thinker" at all... He has taken all culture for his province, and is naturally a little provincial about it: one of the touching things about him is his entire Americanism, an Americanism that could survive unimpaired fifty years in a lunar crater.... If people keep opposing you when you are right, you think them fools; and after a time, right or wrong, you think them fools simply because they oppose you.... The versification of these cantos [LII-LXXI] is interesting: there is none.

Randall Jarrell, in *The New Republic*, December 1940

After Pound's long and rather insolent cultivation of opacity and ambiguity, it would be easy ... to poke fun ... But one must realize that he is in many ways a great figure. He did an extraordinary job thirty years ago of bringing life to English verse, and his influence has not yet petered out. He has written beautiful poetry. That he now sounds less like a poet than like a case history is tragic rather than comic. Faced with these new *Cantos* [LII-LXXI], one's warmest charity is certainly called into play.

Louise Bogan, *A Poet's Alphabet*, p. 336

1941–1945

I should make this distinction about Eliot & Pound—that whatever the essential frivolity & sterility of their critical writing, their poetry itself was a great and creative power.

Archibald MacLeish to Van Wyck Brooks,
20 August 1941

I did not hear the raucous voice from Radio Rome. Friends listened and one especially, whose job it was to check up during the war on the BBC foreign broadcasts, said the effect was baffling, confused, confusing, and she didn't feel that the "message," whatever it was, was doing any harm or good to anybody.

H. D., *End of Torment*, p. 48

What will save him, if anything does, is the fact that no jury on earth could think this kind of drivel would influence anybody to do anything, anywhere, at any time.

Archibald MacLeish to Ernest Hemingway,
27 July 1943

He is obviously crazy.... He has a long history of generosity and unselfish aid to other artists and he is one of the greatest of living poets.

Ernest Hemingway to Archibald MacLeish,
10 August 1943

T. S. Eliot or Ezra Pound or Isadora, irridescent flies caught in the black web of an ancient and amoral European culture. They have in imagination returned to the Europe from which their grandfathers fled, but they have returned to the coffee houses, not the hills.

Sinclair Lewis, *A Sinclair Lewis Reader*, p. 177

What manner of man is Ezra Pound? The answer is a bit of a literary actor and peacock.... He is a master of verbal and metrical expression. His visual and acoustic sensitivity is exquisite. His verse is wonderfully lean . . . [though] to achieve self-expression . . . Pound has always to wear a costume, to enact some role proposed to him by other minds.

Paul Rosenfeld, in *The American Mercury*, January 1944

Now, of course, Pound did not sell himself solely for money. No writer ever does that. . . . But I think it probable that Pound did sell himself partly for prestige, flattery and a professorship.

George Orwell, in *The Tribune*, 28 January 1944

Pound in Rapallo lost himself in one adventitious international "movement" after another, primarily because he did not have the ability to play the single role of Whistler, and was thus far more completely divorced from his audience as a poet and his society as a man. If Whistler was the expatriate as butterfly, Pound was the will-o'-the-wisp.

R. P. Blackmur, *The Lion and the Honeycomb*, p. 73

He suspected that Pound had been the one intellectual indicted for treason only because he had the "guts" to go on saying what his fellows had since decided to keep to themselves.

Bernard DeVoto, quoted in Raymond Nelson,
Van Wyck Brooks, p. 249

A poetic flame, the diving eye of a natural teacher, and a noble personality—part despot, part poet, part press agent.

Time, 1945, quoted in O'Connor and Stone,
A Casebook on Ezra Pound, p. 19

The things that might be said in Pound's defense are things that ought to be carefully thought out. His motives might be significant. Yet, it is entirely possible that Pound deliberately and maliciously undertook to injure this country. Don't you think it worthwhile waiting until you know why he did what he did before rallying to his defense?

Wallace Stevens to Charles Norman, 9 November 1945

I found the poor devil in a rather desperate condition. He is very wobbly in his mind . . . , he flits from one idea to another and is unable to concentrate even to the extent of answering a single question without immediately wandering off the subject.

Julien Cornell to James Laughlin, 20 November 1945

With advancing years his personality, for many years abnormal, has undergone further distortion to the extent that he is now suffering from a paranoid state which renders him mentally unfit . . .

Court medical report, 14 December 1945

1946

The fact that he was so unformidable as a conspirator should not lead us to underrate him as a poet. The fact remains that an important, though frequently mad, writer has returned to his country.

George Dillon, in *Poetry*, September 1946

I can't bear to think of the man, and I can't bear to think of the poet—I mean of his misery. But of course I *have* thought of it continually. I've never allowed anyone to speak against him in my presence.

Edith Sitwell to T. S. Eliot, 4 April 1946

I did see Tom E[liot] at lunch last week, who told me that Ezra's letters are very obviously demented, and very melancholy reading.

Conrad Aiken to Malcolm Cowley, 27 May 1946

I am hoping to get some news from you about Pound. I've been worried by what I've heard, and I wish he could be quietly let out. I don't think that the writers and artists here have behaved terribly well about him.

Edmund Wilson to T. S. Eliot, 15 June 1946

I believe his wits are really very scattered, and he has difficulty in concentrating for more than a few minutes.

Dorothy Pound to Julien Cornell, 14 July 1946

One feels like addressing Pound as Williams addressed the morning star: "Shine alone in the sunrise, towards which you lend no part." . . . Poets of the class in which Pound shines are of an absolute preliminary necessity for the continuing life of poetry.

R. P. Blackmur, in *Poetry*, September 1946

1947

Lowell had long been fascinated by Pound: both by his poetry (although he thought the *Cantos* the "most self-indulgent long poem in English") and by his predicament. . . . He began regularly visiting Pound at St. Elizabeth's and . . . his letters of this time are full of Ezra Pound stories: Pound, he writes to Gertrude Buckman, is "like his later prose and absolutely the most naive and simple man I ever met, sure that the world would be all right if people only read the right books. Pathetic and touching."

Ian Hamilton, *Robert Lowell*, p. 130

Pound was (perhaps is) my friend; & I consider that any human being alive today owes him an immeasurable debt. Why? Not because, as a reformer, he has tried to pry an unworld out of its nonexistence; but because, as a poet, he has created particular beauty in an epoch of universal ugliness.

E. E. Cummings to Julien Cornell, 17 February 1947

Nothing doing about Pound. I should have to saturate myself with his work and I have not the time. Moreover, I never did care to do that sort of critical writing. In Pound's case there would be the special difficulty that he is as persnickety as all hell, if I may say so. A friend has just written to me from France speaking of "My pink Persian cat * * * in front of me, looking up just now with his reproachful amber eyes. He does not like to be molested even by thoughts or looks." That's Pound.

Wallace Stevens to Theodore Weiss,
5 September 1947

1948

Ezra Pound, I feel, is probably a poet of a higher and rarer order than it is easy at all times to realise, because of much irrelevant dust kicked up by his personality as it rushes, strides, or charges across the temporal scene. . . . Pound is— was always, is, must always remain, violently American.

Wyndham Lewis, from *Ezra Pound*,
ed. Peter Russell, pp. 257, 262

Pound's Cantos are the work of a man for whom the thing given has, in general, had the upper hand over deliberation . . . Pound was born to be a workman in verse. . . . At their least valuation I submit that these [Pisan] Cantos in which light and air—and song—move so freely are more exhilirating poetic sketch books . . . than can be found elsewhere in our literature.

Robert Fitzgerald, in *The New Republic*, 16 August 1948

There are notable exceptions. There are fine passages. But the whole [of the *Cantos*] seems to me to be much too disorderly, incomplete, unfinished to be more than a useful text for a biographer.

Reed Whittemore, in *Poetry*, November 1948

In an attempt to take a philosophical attitude . . . , he repeated to himself what Pound had written many years earlier: "It is extremely important that great poetry be written but it is a matter of indifference who writes it." John [Berryman] said he should have this message printed in large letters and hang it over his desk where he would see it every day.

Eileen Simpson, Poets in their Youth, p. 168

1949

By some miracle the Bollingen judges were able to consider Mr. Pound the poet apart from Mr. Pound the fascist, Mr. Pound the anti-Semite, Mr. Pound the traitor, Mr. Pound the funny-money crank, and all the other Mr. Pounds whose existence has properly nothing to do with the question of whether Mr. Pound the poet had or had not written the best American poetry of 1948.

Dwight Macdonald, in Politics, Winter 1949

I agree that the *Pisan Cantos* is Mr. Pound's weakest work, that its selection was a mistake and that the decision reflects glory neither on Mr. Pound nor on the committee. Had I been a Fellow at the time I should have voted against it.... It is sterile where it isn't ugly, intellectually and morally speaking, and ... it is childish to a degree almost never before encountered in a serious work—or one which has been taken seriously.

Archibald MacLeish to Harrison Smith, 27 May 1949,
and to Allen Tate, 15 October 1949

There is [in the *Pisan Cantos*] (amongst a great deal that is quite mad) one perfectly *wonderful* poem ...

Edith Sitwell to John Lehmann, 12 April 1949

My brief criticism of these [Pisan] Cantos remains the words of it. No one in our day has so used the words: they get a new light over them, a new application to the objects, a new *lack* of the stereotyped official use of poetic reference. A new hygiene of the words, cleanliness.

William Carlos Williams, in Imagi, Spring 1949

Despite everything, Pound has an ear for rhythm and an eye for words which assert themselves in every poem. His hatred of an out-moded, literary speech is justified by his own efforts to make words clear and clean and direct. More than this, he makes them move to his own music. . . . [But] this excellent gift for words is applied on the whole to experiences which are dull or distasteful, usually dull. Pound rambles on, without plan or design, about a series of dreary subjects.

C. M. Bowra, in *The New Statesman and Nation*, 3 September 1949

Let us . . . not excuse Pound's political career on the ground that he is a good writer. He *may* be a good writer (I must admit that I personally have always regarded him as an entirely spurious writer), but the opinions that he has tried to disseminate by means of his works are evil ones.

George Orwell, in *Partisan Review*, May 1949

Mr. Pound is incapable of sustained thought in either prose or verse. His acute verbal sensibility is thus at the mercy of random flights of "angelic insight," Icarian self-indulgences . . . [But] as a result of observing Pound's use of language in the past thirty years I had become convinced that he had done more than any other man to regenerate the language, if not the imaginative forms, of English verse.

Allen Tate, *Essays of Four Decades*, pp. 510, 512

Pound the crank is only rarely Pound the poet.

Irving Howe, in *Partisan Review*, May 1949

What is so exasperating about Pound's poetry, for example, is its peculiar combination of a finished technique . . . with amateurish and irresponsible ideas.

Philip Rahv, *Image and Idea*, p. 21

Here, amongst the lunatics, Pound seemed a genial and benevolent host . . .

Stephen Spender, *World Within World*, p. 164

I was glad to see you do something for poor old Pound.

Edmund Wilson to
Louise Bogan, 5 November 1948

The positive, the masculine, and the heroic (or its inversion in satire) are . . . the realm of Pound. . . . [Pound is] typically . . . individualistic, intellectual, aggressive.

Richard Eberhart, in *The Quarterly Review of Literature*, V (1949)

If his critics are right, Pound himself misconceived his work from the beginning and has continued to do so. . . . [But] all the best critics of Pound's work themselves write verse, most of them verse indebted to Pound's, much of it heavily; they have been interested in craft, not personality and subject.

John Berryman, in *Partisan Review*, April 1949

1950

I'll tell you what else I believe: the importance of intensity in art, which is what Pound was saying.

E. E. Cummings, interview,
in *The New York Times*, 31 December 1950

If it is a question of comparing epochs in the work of [Wallace] Stevens and Pound, I do not remember anything in the work of Pound at that period so difficult as many of the poems in this book [*Harmonium*]. Ezra Pound is a naive man, with a few very simple (and sometimes crank) ideas. He has emphatically explained in his prose the themes that he has used in his poetry.

Edmund Wilson to
Harrison Smith, 27 April 1950

Ezra was nice and kind and friendly and a beautiful poet and critic.

Ernest Hemingway to Arthur Mizener, 1 June 1950

1951

The best way for the average student to understand Pound is to assume that he was writing puzzles in poetic form.... It is a scholar's poetry, even if it annoys many scholars. It is a poet's poetry, even if some poets praise the manner rather than the matter.

Earle Davis, in *Kansas Magazine*, 1951

If society indicted and condemned poets for the mixture and the misuse of two great modes of action, poetry and politics, we might have to indict Mr. Pound a second time...

Allen Tate, *Essays of Four Decades*, p. 26

Ezra is convinced that after twenty minutes' instruction in the Georgian dialect, if at the beginning of our difficulties with Russia, Stalin would have given him a five-minute interview, he could have shown the man the error in his thinking, made him see, comprehend, and act on it, and all the subsequent confusion and disaster could have been avoided.

William Carlos Williams,
Autobiography, p. 337

1952

Pound by his translations and critical prefaces has done more perhaps than any living man of letters to create a context of ideas in which poets have been working for some thirty years. Because of Pound that context of contemporary poetry is now world-wide in a sense that it has never been hitherto.

Kathleen Raine, in *The New Republic*, 24 March 1952

Pound is still the old-style optimist, the believer in the good society, which is just around the corner, ready to hand if we only get rid of the financiers and the armament manufacturers and restore order. His own personal tragedy, even, has not brought home to him that he has only scratched the surface of evil, never looked into its depths. He has a beweldered sense of human waste and corruption, but no tragic sense of the human predicament.

Ronald Bottrall, in *The Adelphi*, May 1952

1953

I liked Pound very much. He had this great pretence to universal knowledge and he got to be un-bearable. But the things he did know about he knew very well and he had a lovely heart until he turned bitter.

Ernest Hemingway to Bernard Berenson,
20–22 March 1953

1954

Whatever else we may derive from these essays [*Literary Essays*]—and Pound's comments are often of the greatest interest—the lack of centrality and the lack of any complete conception of tradition cannot but point us to the absence of the discipline of an organic literary-critical approach ... [, though he] began in greatness and with a passionate concern for the direction of European culture.

Charles Tomlinson, in *The Spectator*, 19 February 1954

Pound is quite unreliable, not just in matters of fact, but precisely in matters of judgment.... He really needs all the allowances that can be made for him ... but how far should one go in giving the benefit of the doubt?

Donald Davie, in *The New Statesman and Nation*,
27 March 1954

Above all, Pound is an American. His interest in literature, in certain writers he particularly values, is sometimes a proprietary interest. [Yet] it is from Pound...that the hard, sharp critical view has stemmed during the last thirty years.

Roy Fuller, in *The London Magazine*, May 1954

On the question as to which American authors our readers would like to see represented, the vote [by questionnaire] was not expected save in one case. The poet Ezra Pound received as many requests as several of the more popular novelists. In fact he was the only poet to attain a place in their favoured company.

Editorial, unsigned, in *Perspectives*, Autumn 1954

I am not conscious of having been influenced by anybody and have purposely held off reading highly mannered people like Eliot and Pound so that I should not absorb anything, even unconsciously.

Wallace Stevens to Richard Eberhart, 15 January 1954

1955

Old Ezra Pound...is often a fool...who can so disgust me sometimes with his antisemitism and childish fascism that I cannot write to him; but was never a knave and often an excellent poet with all his pretensions[. He] now writes me exclusively in what I can best describe as Unknown Tongue.

Ernest Hemingway to Bernard Berenson, 24 October 1955

Pound, even in his later years and in his continuing tragic situation, has kept one part of his work free from the rigidity of dogma; the fluidity of poetry keeps breaking into the fixed design.... The *Cantos*, however, now [seem] slightly fossilized—worthy of note as origin and as process but with no truly invigorating aspects.

Louise Bogan, *A Poet's Alphabet*, pp. 339, 341

1956

You are our greatest living poet; a small distinction but your own.

> Ernest Hemingway to Ezra Pound, 19 July 1956

A great deal of the book [*Rock-Drill Cantos*] is interesting in the way an original soul's indiscriminate notes ... are interesting; ... if you had read exactly the books Pound has read, known exactly the people Pound has known, and felt about it exactly as Pound has felt, you could understand the Cantos pretty well. Gertrude Stein was most unjust to Pound when she called that ecumenical alluder a village explainer: he can hardly even tell you anything (unless you know it already), much less explain it. He makes notes on the margin of the universe; to tell how just or unjust a note is, you must know that portion of the text yourself.

> Randall Jarrell, in
> *The Yale Review*, September 1956

The details, especially in the earlier Cantos, are frequently very lovely, but since there is neither structure nor very much in the way of meaning, the details are details and nothing more, and what we have is the ghost of poetry, though I am willing to admit that it is often the ghost of great poetry.

> Yvor Winters, *The Function of Criticism*, p. 47

Most contemporary critics are conspicuous by their ability to cope with Pound's Cantos.

> Noel Stock, in *Meanjin*, March 1956

1957

His integrity and courage as an artist is unequalled. He is still *il miglior fabbro*.

> A. Alvarez, in *The Observer*, 3 March 1957

Those many readers who wrote off Pound in the Thirties and were persuaded to give him a second chance, because of some poignant and direct passages in the *Pisan Cantos*, can now write him off again.... Either this is the waste of a prodigious talent, or else it is the poetry of the future.

Donald Davie, in *The New Statesman and Nation*, 9 March 1957

Please let me make something onceforall clear: from my standpoint, not EEC [himself] but EP [Ezra Pound] is the authentic "innovator"; the true trailblazer of an epoch; "this selfstyled world's greatest and most generous literary figure"—nor shall I ever forget the thrill I experienced on first reading "The Return"

E. E. Cummings to Charles Norman, 1957

If I was ever cross with you it was for leaving America behind too far and Ezra not far enough.

Robert Frost to T. S. Eliot, 2 May 1957

I should hate to see Ezra die ignominiously in that wretched place where he is for a crime which if proven couldn't have kept him all these years in prison.... I suppose we might be prepared to answer for Ezra's relative sanity ... [though] neither you nor I would want to take him into our family or even into our neighborhood.

Robert Frost to Archibald MacLeish, 24 June 1957

He has books, everything; students come to me in Paris and tell me about him. *Fascist*. Those dreadful people he knows ...

Sylvia Beach, quoted from H. D., *End of Torment*, p. 34

To receive his disapproval was to find a long, red-scored envelope on the breakfast table. A good cup of coffee and we could face it. There is little bite under his bluster.

Patricia Hutchins, *Ezra Pound's Kensington*, p. 22

1958

What Pound also took from the 'Nineties, or from Whistler at least, was a belief in the importance of *poetry as picture* ... Color, composition or form, and above all else visual perception, are the elements which were increasingly important to him.

Earl Miner, *The Japanese Tradition in British and American Poetry*, p. 110

So you think Ezra Pound needs rehabilitating? Allow me to disagree. If the man has sinned, nothing you can say or do will make him sinless—and if you're trying to render the poet socially respectable, that's an insult ... In this UNworld of "ours", lots of UNpoets and plenty of UNcountries (UNamerica, for example) need rehabilitating the very worst way. But whoever or whatever he may be, Ezra Pound emphatically isn't UNanyone or UNanything.

E. E. Cummings to a group of Swiss correspondents, 18 August 1958

Read Pound aloud and was rapt.

The Journals of Sylvia Plath, p. 290

Tuesday was an event! I went to New York to see Ezra and Dorothy off. There on the boat lay Ezra, stripped to the waist, his torso rather proudly sunburned. ... Ezra was no different from ever. For half an hour he lectured me on college entrance examinations, and the program I must follow to improve them. ... Ezra took both my hands and pressed them warmly. ... "Don't look so sad," [he] said.

Norman Holmes Pearson, quoted in H. D., *End of Torment*, p. 62

He went very wrongheaded in his egotism ... He has never admitted that he went over to the enemy ... I hate such nonsense and can only listen to it as an evidence of mental disorder. But ... Ezra Pound is not too dangerous to go free in his wife's care, and [is] too insane ever to be tried.

Robert Frost, court statement, 18 April 1958

The main thing about Ezra Pound is that he is a poet of towering gifts and attainments.

Richard H. Rovere, court statement, 18 April 1958

There are very few living poets, even if they are not conscious of having been influenced by Pound, who could say, "My work would be exactly the same if Mr. Pound had never lived."

W. H. Auden, court statement, 18 April 1958

1960

Through the years Pound has remembered a great deal, but he has learned nothing.... The new Cantos [*de los Cantares*] have many interesting passages, some passages of unique lyrical beauty, and too many passages when inspiration and excited self-indulgence have been confused with one another.... Nevertheless it must immediately be added that what is bad and self-indulgent...is inseparable from Pound's poetic genius at its best.

Delmore Schwartz, in *The New Republic*,
8 February 1960

I intend...no disrespect to the Cantos or their author when I say [perfectly seriously] that the best state to get into before reading them is a state of trance.... The real mistake, in my opinion, is made by those critics who see the Cantos as a logical, lucid, carefully worked-out problem in literary engineering.

John Wain, in *The Spectator*, 11 March 1960

Eliot has developed and argued Pound's insights so that they are believed by critics and professors; it was Pound who originated them for poets.... [But] Pound is not only the cause of poetry in other men. He is a great poet, and the Cantos are his master work.

Donald Hall, in *The New Statesman
and Nation*, 12 March 1960

126

Pound's phrase-flash technique...never permits us to have thoughts—only to memorize a certain number of incidents as examples of a pre-fixed meaning. It is like having one's meat pre-chewed by a solicitious mother...

W. D. Snodgrass, in
Hudson Review, Spring 1960

By now the Cantos can be seen to express a comprehensive vision, almost a mystical one, of human life as a part of total reality.

John Holloway, in
The London Magazine, June 1960

1961–1972

Ezra Pound's poetry is most admired for the beauty of its sound... Still, if his poetry sounds that good, and if the sense it makes is often inoffensive and sometimes good, then why is he so actively resisted?... [Because] Pound's been over-sold....Quite apart from the poet's historical importance, [even his best poetry] is exquisite and technically masterful, but slight in its impact.

George P. Elliott, in *The Carleton Miscellany*,
Summer 1961

Pound as a schoolmaster is sometimes given credit for being more original than he in fact was....As a poet in his own right, he was less impressive than as a teacher.

Malcolm Cowley, in *The Reporter*, 2 March 1961

I doubted then and do doubt that Ezra Pound was ever for a moment insane. He was just a complete, natural phenomenon of Unreason.

Notebook entry, 1965,
The Collected Essays of Katherine Anne Porter

Pound's ideas are responsible for most of the good writing in verse in the 20th century, and for a good deal of the prose too.... Whenever I am tempted to criticize Pound harshly, as I am whenever I have to read the Cantos, I think of ... what poetry would be like today if Pound had not existed. Above all, he gave us a language to write in.... [Yet] Pound was not a great poet ... [and] in the Cantos you can see most clearly what Pound lacked—an identity. He had ideas, he had an excellent gift of mimicry ... but he never had a center of his own. And he was oddly naive, unable to think beyond appearances.

Louis Simpson, in *Book Week*, 2 January 1966

The farther his viewpoint ranges afield, the more his style falls into the phony dialect and the analphabetic spelling of the Yankee cracker-barrel philosopher. His *Cantos* are ... a babel of archaism, genealogies, misquotations, mistranslations, smutty jokes, and purely decorative ideograms, eked out with powerful and poignant lyrical fragments which graduate students will be piecing together for years to come, in compensation for that brief academic career which he interrupted but never quite lived down.

Harry Levin, *Refractions*, p. 79

Pound is the leader, at the very forefront.... One is inclined to say everything comes from him.

Hayden Carruth, in *Poetry*, May 1967

Pound ... [is] the creator of modern verse translation as of so much else.

D. S. Carne-Ross, in *Delos* 1, 1966

The new set of scraps from Ezra Pound [*Drafts and Fragments of Cantos CX-CXVII*] is ... strictly for devotees. Even the fullest of these drafts for further Cantos are not so much mutterings as mumblings.

Derwent May, in *The Observer*, 15 March 1970

For all of Pound's influence upon the profession of poetry, his work has scarcely affected the general public, although certain attitudes and linguistic devices have passed through lesser poets to the larger audience. (Some of this circuitous intellectual influence has been lamentable, because neither Pound's thought nor his poetry are especially wise.)...Rare is the contemporary poet who can write more than twenty pages without appropriating Poundian compositional devices ... [but] more bad poetry in America today is indebted to Pound than anyone else.

Richard Kostelanetz, *The Old
Poetics and the New*, pp. 49–51

As for Pound, of course, a lot of his things stay in one's mind forever. Again, I have a great many reservations about Pound.... Pound's ego system, Pound's organization of the world around a character, a kind of masculine energy, is extremely foreign to me.... What I really read in Pound are passages and lines. Just about the time I'm beginning to consider Pound an idiot, I come to something ... and I know that I'm reading a very great poet.

George Oppen, in *The Contemporary Writer*,
ed. L. S. Dembro and Cyrena Pondrom, p. 183

First, I had better admit that I believe that Pound's critical writing ... is an absolute foundation stone of contemporary American writing. But in his own work I think he's been disastrous as a model, totally disastrous to younger writers.

Carl Rakosi, in *The Contemporary Writer*, p. 193

I think we are all agreed that the term "objectivism," as we understood Pound's use of it, corresponded to the way we felt poetry should be written.

Charles Reznikoff, in
The Contemporary Writer, p. 210

Williams came along and said, "No, we've got to get a new poetic foot," and while he did wonderful things instinctively, I wish he had omitted some of the theory. Pound was more sensible.

Louis Zukofsky, in The Contemporary Writer, p. 227

He is, unquestionably, the single greatest influence on modern poetry in English in this century, but there is considerable question about his own status as a poet. Leaving aside his translations it is hard to name a single poem of his which will stand up as a poem. Maybe *Hugh Selwyn Mauberley*—but only maybe.... As poet he is simply not in the same class as Yeats. After all, the work of a poet is to make *poems*.

Archibald MacLeish to
Ranald H. Macdonald, Jr.,
March 1972

After I was *in* Eliot's poems Pound began to make sense ...

Allen Tate, Essays of Four Decades, p. 226

Greatest poet of the age.... The one poet who heard speech as spoken from the actual body and began to measure it to lines that could be chanted rhythmically without violating human common sense ..., the first poet to open up fresh new forms in America after Walt Whitman—certainly the greatest poet since Walt Whitman ... The Cantos were for the first time a single person registering over the course of a lifetime all of his major obsessions and thoughts ...

Allen Ginsberg, radio interview,
St. Louis, Missouri, 1 November 1972

Ezra was kinder and more Christian about people than I was. His own writing, when he would hit it right, was so perfect, and he was so sincere in his mistakes and so enamored of his errors, and so kind to people that I always thought of him as a sort of saint.

Ernest Hemingway, A Moveable Feast, p. 108

Ezra Pound has stood accused of fake erudition; of wanton misunderstanding of such matters as Chinese poetics; of imposing values by the sheerest assertion. . . . Pound knew less than he wanted to, and often, through impetuosity, less than he thought he did; Pound imposed by the sheer authority of his manner; Pound had better not be one's mentor, beyond appeal, on questions of scholarly fact. But he believed, with purity of heart, in what he was doing.

Hugh Kenner, A Homemade World, p. 12

Books Cited

Atlas, James. *Delmore Schwartz*. New York: Farrar, Straus & Giroux, 1977; reprint edition, New York: Avon, 1978.

Auden, W. H. *The Dyer's Hand*. New York: Random House, 1962.

_____. *Secondary Worlds*. New York: Random House, 1968

Autobiography of William Carlos Williams. New York: New Directions, 1951.

Axelrod, Steven Gould. *Robert Lowell, Life and Art*. Princeton: Princeton University Press, 1979.

Baker, Carlos. *Ernest Hemingway*. New York: Scribner's, 1969.

_____, ed. *Ernest Hemingway: Selected Letters, 1917–1961*. New York: Scribner's, 1981.

Ball, Gordon, ed. *Allen Verbatim*. New York: McGraw-Hill, 1974.

Bateson, F. W. *A Guide to English Literature*. Garden City: Anchor, 1968.

Berryman, John. *The Freedom of the Poet*. New York: Farrar, Straus & Giroux, 1976.

Blackmur, R. P. *The Lion and the Honeycomb*. New York: Harcourt, Brace & World, 1955.

Bode, Carl. *Mencken*. Carbondale: Southern Illinois University Press, 1969.

Bogan, Louise. *A Poet's Alphabet*. New York: McGraw-Hill, 1970.

Boulton, James T., ed. *Lawrence in Love: Letters From D. H. Lawrence to Louie Burrows*. Nottingham: University of Nottingham Press, 1968.

Braybrooke, Neville, ed. *The Ackerley Letters*. New York: Harcourt Brace Jovanovich, 1975.

Brooks, Cleanth. *A Shaping Joy*. New York: Harcourt Brace Jovanovich, 1971.

The Cantos of Ezra Pound; Some Testimonies. New York: Farrar and Rinehart, 1933.

Churchill, Allen. *The Improper Bohemians*. New York: Dutton, 1959.

Cummings, E. E. *A Miscellany Revised*. New York: October House, 1965.

Dahlberg, Edward. *Epitaphs of Our Times: the letters of Edward Dahlberg*. New York: Braziller, 1967.

Darroch, Sandra Jobson. *Ottoline*. New York: Coward, McCann & Geoghegan, 1975.

Davie, Michael, ed. *The Diaries of Evelyn Waugh*. Boston: Little, Brown, 1976.

Dembo, L. S. and Cyrena N. Pondrom, eds. *The Contemporary Writer*. Madison: University of Wisconsin Press, 1972.

Duncan, Ronald. *All Men Are Islands*. London: R. Hart-Davis, 1964.

Dupee, F. W. and George Stade, eds. *Selected Letters of E. E. Cummings*. New York: Harcourt, Brace and World, 1969.

Eliot, T. S. *To Criticize the Critic*. New York: Farrar, Straus & Giroux, 1965.

Ellmann, Richard, ed. *Selcted Letters of James Joyce*. New York: Viking, 1975.

Fitzgibbon, Constantine, ed. *Selected Letters of Dylan Thomas*. London: Dent, 1966.

————. *The Life of Dylan Thomas*. Boston: Little, Brown, 1965.

Forgue, Guy J., ed. *Letters of H. L. Mencken*. New York: Knopf, 1961; reprint edition, Boston: Northeast University Press, 1981.

Frost, Robert. *The Letters of Robert Frost to Louis Untermeyer*. New York: Holt, Rinehart and Winston, 1963.

Fuller, Edmund, ed. *Journey Into the Self, Being the Letters, Papers, and Journals of Leo Stein*. New York: Crown, 1950.

Gordon, Lyndall. *Eliot's Early Years*. New York: Oxford University Press, 1977.

Gould, Jean. *Amy*. New York: Dodd, Mead, 1975.

Grade, Arnold, ed. *Family Letters of Robert and Elinor Frost*. Albany: State University of New York Press, 1972.

Green, Julian. *Diary, 1928–1957*. New York: Harcourt, Brace & World, 1964.

Greenberg, Clement. *Art and Culture*. Boston: Beacon, 1961.

Gregory, Horace. *Amy Lowell*. New York: Nelson, 1958.

————. *The House on Jefferson Street: A Cycle of Memories*. New York: Holt, Rinehart and Winston, 1971.

Hamilton, Ian. *Robert Lowell*. New York: Random House, 1982.

H. D., *End to Torment: A Memoir of Ezra Pound*. New York: New Directions, 1979.

Hemingway, Ernest. *A Moveable Feast*. New York: Scribner's, 1964; reprint edition, New York: Bantam, 1965.

Heymann, C. David. *Ezra Pound: The Last Rower*. New York: Viking, 1976.

Holroyd, Michael. *Lytton Strachey*, 2 vols. New York: Holt, Rinehart and Winston, 1967.

Homberger, Eric, ed. *Ezra Pound: The Critical Heritage*. London: Routledge and Kegan Paul, 1972.

Hughes, Michael, ed. *The Letters of Lewis Mumford and Frederic J. Osborn*. New York: Praeger, 1972.

Hutchins, Patricia. *Ezra Pound's Kensington*. London: Faber and Faber, 1965.

Jepson, Edgar. *Memories of an Edwardian*. London: Secker, 1938.

Josephson, Matthew. *Life Among the Surrealists*. New York: Holt, Rinehart and Winston, 1962.

Kenner, Hugh. *A Homemade World*. New York: Knopf, 1975; reprint edition, New York, Morrow, 1975.

Keynes, Geoffrey, ed. *The Letters of Rupert Brooke*. New York: Harcourt, Brace & World, 1968.

Killorin, Joseph, ed. *Selected Letters of Conrad Aiken*. New Haven: Yale University Press, 1978.

Kostelanetz, Richard. *The Old Poetries and the New*. Ann Arbor: University of Michigan Press, 1981.

Laughlin, James [S. D.] *Notes on Ezra Pound's Cantos*, pamphlet insert in Ezra Pound, *Cantos LII-LXXV*. Norfolk, Conn.: New Directions, 1940.

Lawrence, T. E. *The Letters of T. E. Lawrence*. New York: Doubleday, Doran, 1939.

Leavis, F. R. *New Bearings in English Poetry*. London: Chatto & Windus, 1932; reprint edition, Harmondsworth: Penguin, 1963.

Leavis, F. R. and Q. D. Leavis. *Lectures in America*. London: Chatto & Windus, 1969.

Levin, Harry. *Refractions*. New York: Oxford University Press, 1966.

Lewis, C. Day. *The Poetic Image*. London: Jonathan Cape, 1947.

Lewis, R. W. B. *Edith Wharton*. New York: Harper & Row, 1975.

Lewis, Sinclair. *A Sinclair Lewis Reader: The Man from Main Street: Selected Essays and Other Writings, 1904–1950*. New York: Random House, 1953; reprint edition, New York: Pocket Books, 1963.

Lewis, Thomas S. W., ed. *Letters of Hart Crane and His Family*. New York: Columbia University Press, 1974.

Lindberg-Seyersted, Brita, ed. *Pound/Ford, The Story of a Literary Friendship: The Correspondence Between Ezra Pound and Ford Madox Ford and Their Writings About Each Other*. New York: New Directions, 1982.

Ludington, Townsend, ed. *The Fourteenth Chronicle: Letters and Diaries of John Dos Passos*. Boston: Gambit, 1973.

Maas, Henry, ed. *The Letters of A. E. Housman*. London: R. Hart-Davis, 1971.

McHugh, Roger, ed. *Ah, Sweet Dancer: W. B. Yeats and Margot Ruddock*. New York: Macmillan, 1970.

Miner, Earl. *The Japanese Tradition in British and American Literature*. Princeton: Princeton University Press, 1958.

Mitgang, Herbert, ed. *The Letters of Carl Sandburg*. New York: Harcourt, Brace & World, 1968.

Monro, Harold. *Some Contemporary Poets*. London: L. Parsons, 1920.

Murphy, William M. *Prodigal Father: The Life of John Butler Yeats (1839–1922)*. Ithaca: Cornell University Press, 1978.

Nelson, Raymond. *Van Wyck Brooks*. New York: Dutton, 1981.

Nicolson, Nigel, and Joanne Trautmann, eds. *The Letters of Virginia Woolf*, 6 vols. New York: Harcourt Brace Jovanovich, 1975–1980.

Norman, Charles. *The Case of Ezra Pound*. New York: Funk and Wagnalls, 1968.

————. E. E. Cummings. Boston: Little, Brown, 1972.

O'Connor, William and Edward Stone, *A Casebook on Ezra Pound* New York: Crowell, 1959.

Olson, Charles. *Human Universe and Other Essays*. New York: Grove, 1967.

Olson, Stanley. *Elinor Wylie*. New York: Dial, 1979.

Orwell, George. *The Collected Essays, Journalism and Letters*, 4 vols. London: Secker & Warburg, 1968; reprint edition, Harmondsworth: Penguin, 1970.

Perkins, George, ed. *American Poetic Theory*. New York: Holt, Rinehart, and Winston, 1972.

Plath, Sylvia. *The Journals of Sylvia Plath*. New York: Dial, 1982.

———. *Letters Home*. New York: Harper & Row, 1975.

Porter, Katherine Anne. *The Collected Essays and Occasional Writings of Katherine Anne Porter*. New York: Delacorte, 1970.

Putzel, Max. *The Man in the Mirror: William Marion Reedy and His Magazine*. Cambridge: Harvard University Press, 1963.

Rachewiltz, Mary de. *Discretions*. Boston: Little, Brown, 1971.

Rahv, Philip. *Essays on Literature and Politics, 1932–1972*. Boston: Houghton Mifflin, 1978.

———. *Image and Idea*. New York: New Directions, 1957.

Reid, B. L. *The Man From New York: John Quinn and His Friends*. New York: Oxford University Press, 1968.

Ross, Robert H. *The Georgian Revolt, 1910–1922*. Carbondale: Southern Illinois University Press, 1965.

Russell, Peter, ed. *An Examination of Ezra Pound: A Collection of Essays To Be Presented To Ezra Pound On His 65th Birthday*. Norfolk, Conn.: New Directions, 1950.

Seager, Allen. *The Glass House: The Life of Theodore Roethke*. New York: McGraw-Hill, 1968.

Seferis, George. *On the Greek Style*. London: Bodley Head, 1967.

Simpson, Eileen. *Poets in Their Youth*. New York: Random House, 1982.

Stiwell, Edith. *Selected Letters, 1919–1964*. New York: Vanguard, 1970.

Smith, Grover, ed. *Letters of Aldous Huxley*. New York: Harper & Row, 1969.

Sparrow, John. *Sense and Poetry*. London: Constable, 1934.

Spender, Stephen. *World Within World*. London: Hamish Hamilton, 1951.

Stevens, Holly, ed. *Letters of Wallace Stevens*. New York: Knopf, 1966.

Stock, Noel. *The Life of Ezra Pound*. San Francisco: North Point, 1982.

Tate, Allen. *Essays of Four Decades*. Chicago: Swallow, 1968.

Thomas, Edward. *Letters from Edward Thomas to Gordon Bottomley*. New York: Oxford University Press, 1968.

Thompson, Lawrence, ed. *Selected Letters of Robert Frost*. New York: Holt, Rinehart and Winston, 1964.

Tillyard, E. M. W. *Poetry Direct and Oblique*. London: Chatto & Windus, 1934; reprint edition, 1945.

Tindall, William York. *The Literary Symbol*. New York: Columbia University Press, 1955; reprint edition, Madison: University of Wisconsin Press, 1962.

Turnbull, Andrew, ed. *The Letters of F. Scott Fitzgerald*. New York: Scribner's, 1963; reprint edition, New York: Dell, 1965.

Ure, Peter. *W. B. Yeats*. Edinburgh: Oliver and Boyd, 1963; reprint edition, New York: Grove, 1964.

Weber, Brom, ed. *The Letters of Hart Crane*. Berkeley: University of California Press, 1965.

Weintraub, Stanley. *The London Yankees*. New York: Harcourt Brace Jovanovich, 1979.

Wickes, George, ed. *Lawrence Durrell and Henry Miller: A Private Correspondence*. New York: Dutton, 1964.

Wilkinson, Marguerite. *New Voices*. New York: Macmillan, 1921.

Williams, Ellen. *Harriet Monroe and the Poetry Renaissance*. Urbana: University of Illinois Press, 1977.

Williams, William Carlos. *The Selected Letters of William Carlos Williams*. New York: McDowell, Obolensky, 1957.

Wilson, Edmund. *Letters on Literature and Politics, 1912–1972*. New York: Farrar, Straus and Giroux, 1977.

_____. *The Shores of Light*. New York: Random House, 1952; reprint edition, New York: Vintage, 1961.

Winsatt, W. K. *Day of the Leopards*. New Haven: Yale University Press, 1976.

_____. *Hateful Contraries*. Lexington: University of Kentucky Press, 1966.

_____. *The Verbal Icon*. Lexington: University of Kentucky Press, 1954.

Wimsatt, W. K. and Cleanth Brooks. *Literary Criticism: A Short History*. New York: Knopf, 1965.

Winnick, R. H., ed. *Letters of Archibald MacLeish, 1907 to 1982.* Boston: Houghton Mifflin, 1983.

Winters, Yvor. *In Defense of Reason.* Chicago: Swallow, n.d.

———. *The Function of Criticism.* Denver: Swallow, 1957.

Yeats, W. B. *A Packet for Ezra Pound.* Dublin: Cuala Press, 1929.

———. *Letters on Poetry from W. B. Yeats to Dorothy Wellesley.* London: Oxford University Press, 1964.

———, ed. *Oxford Book of Modern Verse.* Oxford: Oxford University Press, 1936.

———. *Selected Criticism,* ed. A. Norman Jeffares. London: Macmillan, 1964.

Zabel, Morton Dauwen, ed. *Literary Opinion in America.* New York: Harper & Brothers, 1951.

Index

Originators of the statements here collected: